RAISING THE EXCEPTIONAL CHILD

Raising the Exceptional Child

Michael T. Yura, PH.D.
Lawrence Zuckerman, ED.D.

HAWTHORN BOOKS, INC.
Publishers/New York
A Howard & Wyndham Company

RAISING THE EXCEPTIONAL CHILD

Library of Congress Catalog Card Number: 79-63620
ISBN: 0-8015-6220-1

10 9 8 7 6 5 4 3 2 1

793525

To our wives and children

CONTENTS

Contents

Section Four

POSITIVE PARENTAL ATTITUDES

Section Five

FAMILY ATMOSPHERE

Section Six

APPENDIXES

PREFACE

In recent years there has been an extensive movement toward educating parents in various child-rearing methods. This movement has gathered momentum because of the increasing need for more effective parenting skills. As parents are confronted with the everyday difficulties of raising children, they find themselves in situations they are ill prepared to deal with, particularly an increasing amount of rebellion. The parenting techniques found effective in the past are no match for the challenges of today.

In the current movement of parent education there is a group of parents who have been forgotten about, yet who are in great need of the same type of assistance in dealing with their children—the parents of exceptional children. They have for a long time been neglected, left on their own to adapt various basic child-rearing techniques to their unique situations. We hope by writing this book to assist parents in meeting the challenge of parenting an exceptional child.

Although the word *exceptional* refers to any variation from the norm, we are directing our attention to those children who exhibit physiological and intellectual dysfunctions. But the purpose of this book is not only to describe the disabilities of exceptional children, but also to help all parents of exceptional children gain a practical and systematic overall approach to dealing with their children's misbehavior. The democratic techniques of family living that are presented are applicable to the other children in the family as well. The parenting concepts presented in this book have been adapted from the contributions Alfred Adler and Rudolf Dreikurs have made in the development of understanding human behavior.

We have organized this book in five progressive steps. The information discussed in the first section lays the groundwork for the better understanding of the second section. This process of building upon previously learned knowledge ensures the reader of the fullest integration of the various child-rearing techniques presented.

To help parents master the principles set forth, we have provided a learning activities workbook (see Appendix 1). Parents also can refer to this for a programmed approach to the book. Appendix 2 is a further guide for parent study groups.

The maximizing of the parents' understanding of democratic principles helps develop independent living skills in exceptional children. It is the parents' ability to foster mutual respect and a sense of equality in the family that provides situations to foster the growth of independence, while at the same time developing a harmonious relationship between parent and child.

The authors wish to give special thanks to Mary Jane Betz for her encouragement and support given us in undertaking the development of this material.

A special thank-you is extended by the authors to Shelia Stephens Newman for her valuable technical assistance provided in the development of this manuscript. We wish to thank Johanna Faber and Valerie Zuckerman for their time and effort put into the screening of material used in the appendixes of this book. Appreciation is extended to Margaret Lopez and Ann Cloonan for the typing of this manuscript. Our heartfelt thanks is also extended to all the parents who shared their special needs with us, which in turn allowed us to broaden our knowledge of exceptional children.

Basic Principles in Understanding Child Development

1

CHILD REARING IN
OUR CONTEMPORARY SOCIETY

We are living in a decade where a great emphasis has been placed on developing materials and programs in the area of parent education. We are all aware that there have been numerous parenting methods promoted over the past few years. We can walk into almost any bookstore and find an entire section devoted to how to raise and care for our children. Why have so many books appeared recently for parents describing new approaches to raising children? There is a need for these parent education books, evidenced by the increased numbers that appear each year on the bookshelves. What has created this need?

In the past parents followed traditional child-rearing methods they learned from their parents that were supported by societal attitudes. The sayings "Children should be seen and not heard" and "Children should do as I say and not as I do" both communicate the general theme of traditional child-rearing methods. These phrases communicate parental authority; parents give the orders and children obey. It is clear from these two statements what children *should* and *should not* do. Because autocratic methods at one time were supported by our society, they worked effectively for parents. A child would never have dreamed of being late for dinner or refusing to perform a household chore if told to do so. Tradition set the stage for what was expected from children and how parents were to deal with their children. If

3

children disobeyed, they would feel the wrath of their parents. Rather than face punitive measures, most children listened. Parents erroneously viewed this obedience as respect. In actuality children did what they were told out of fear of punishment.

Children who obeyed out of fear no more respected their parents than children who were openly defiant. If children learned anything, it was not to respect their parents but rather to fear power and authority or to use power for their own benefit. The use of power worked in the past because societal attitudes supported parental authority. Society was not concerned with developing relationships based on equality. Relationships ranged from dominant to submissive or from superior to inferior. This is no longer true. Today societal attitudes are different. Autocratic methods of child rearing are outdated and ineffective. People are concerned with their own equality, and are therefore socially aware of the needs and rights of others. If parents try to impose their authority upon children today, they will only meet with resistance. Feeling societal equality, children now refuse to be dominated and rebel against parental pressures.

As parents realized that the typical constraints placed upon children were no longer effective but in fact increased the rebelliousness of children, they attempted to win cooperation and discourage rebelliousness by easing constraints. They went from one extreme, autocracy, to the other extreme, permissiveness. But it does not take parents long to learn that permissive measures lead to total disruption. The respect for individual rights is overlooked when people believe they have the freedom to do as they please, that individuals do not need to be responsible for their actions. This in turn negates any respect for order. However, permissiveness is very different from the freedom in democracy. In a democratic society freedom also entails a responsibility both to act in a manner that shows respect for the rights of others and to ensure respect for order. In a permissive society one does as one pleases only to benefit oneself. In a democratic society the responsible individual conforms to the needs of the situation to benefit everyone involved.

Parents are concerned with developing this sense of responsibility in their children but find themselves caught in a dilemma. They swing back and forth as though hanging on a pendulum, moving from autocratic practices to permissiveness. Mother has already told Johnny that he cannot have any snacks since dinner will be served soon. Johnny begins to whine and demand that he be allowed to have his snack. Johnny's whining is so persistent that out of frustration, mother finally says, "What's the use?" and gives in to Johnny's demand. Mother's assertion of parental authority didn't carry any weight and she eventually resorted to permissiveness. Neither approach appears to be an effective training method.

Without traditional guidelines of raising children or the knowledge of democratic principles for family living, parents become confused. How do they deal with their children? Can they establish discipline through democratic means? The numerous parenting books and parent education programs offered today try to fill this existing need in the hope of putting an end to the dilemma of contemporary parenting.

It is possible to develop an egalitarian family atmosphere and a positive relationship with children while at the same time establishing discipline. First we need to understand the role democracy has played in parent-child relationships.

Our society is built on the democratic belief that all people are created equal and have the same human rights of respect and dignity. This belief has recently received more and more support. Individuals can no longer be legally discriminated against because of race, religion, ethnic origin, sex, age, or physical limitations. Our country is moving in a direction that promotes the treatment of all individuals as equals and no longer supports autocratic, superior-inferior relationships. Our children do not live in a vacuum and are very much affected by these trends. Children, like other groups of individuals, wish to be treated and dealt with in a mutually respectful manner. When Sally refuses to eat her dinner and begins crying at the dinner table, mother need not try to force Sally to eat or make a special meal for Sally. Mother would only be disrespectful if she were to use threats and would lose her own self-respect if she were to cater to Sally's every desire. Mother can simply inform Sally in a firm and pleasant manner, "This is what we have for dinner and you can choose to eat it or not, but if you continue to misbehave at the table, you will have to leave until you can behave properly." Mother has taken a firm stand, has maintained her self-respect, and has shown respect toward Sally by remaining pleasant. Mutual respect has been achieved.

There has been a surge of energy throughout our country to increase the practice of equality and democracy. This has created a social awareness of and an atmosphere conducive to human rights. It has been this movement toward the true practice of equality that has made traditional and autocratic child-rearing practices ineffective. Children realize that they do not have to play the role of second best. Parents may strongly disagree with the theory of child equality, but they can no longer place themselves in a superior position to their children and expect to maintain an harmonious relationship. The equality of children does not mean they have the same capabilities as their parents. It does mean that parents and children need to develop relationships based upon mutual respect. A five-year-old child and a thirty-year-old adult are entitled to the same human rights.

As parents we have the responsibility of guiding our children. However, some of us mistakenly believe that we can only guide and discipline our children through domination. No longer can we force, threaten, or demand that our children do what we say and expect positive results. We need to learn methods of encouragement and ways of understanding our children if we are to aid them in developing a sense of independence, cooperation, and responsibility. Democratic parenting principles are essential ingredients for establishing a mutually respectful relationship and are necessary in our present society to guide our children effectively.

The trends toward a more equal system of government, opportunity, and education have just begun to be felt by parents of children who have some type of limitation or handicap. These parents have now begun to reevaluate their method of child rearing and maintaining a sense of discipline with their children. The child-rearing practices of parents of exceptional children are going through a similar transition to that which parents in general have been experiencing. The main difference is that the parents of exceptional children also have to contend with certain societal attitudes that greatly affect their parenting procedures.

For years exceptional children were treated as "different." The parental attitudes tended toward seeing the child as being incapable of "normal" living even if he had training. Many children were institutionalized because they were different. The general feeling was that being different was bad. Parents termed the child who had learning problems as retarded or lazy, without making an attempt at a true understanding of her unique difficulty. Discrimination against the handicapped child existed in all phases of life—school, work, and family. This discrimination limited opportunity for growth as well as discouraged special skill training. Thus, exceptional children were kept out of the mainstream of life.

Societal attitudes greatly influenced how children were treated and thought of in the home. Autocratic child-rearing methods paralleled autocratic societal attitudes. The inequality that once existed between parents and children in general was mirrored in the inequality of treatment and opportunity afforded exceptional children. But as our society has moved away from autocracy toward more democratic practices that have affected parents' methods, there has been a great transition in its attitude toward the exceptional child as well.

The emphasis in a more democratic society is one toward equality, ensuring that each individual has the right to fulfill his own human potential. Societal attitudes have recently begun to emphasize equality in our dealing with exceptional persons. The right to access of public buildings and the right to an equal educational opportunity are two of the monumental changes that have grown out of the overall movement toward more democratic practices in our society. We now need to apply these democratic principles to exceptional children. We have begun to accept the principle of equal treatment for a child in our society. The exceptional child must now also experience this feeling of equality in the context of how parents deal with her As a result of this conviction, a movement has recently developed to train large numbers of parents of exceptional children in democratic child-rearing methods.

Since autocratic methods have proved ineffective in a democratic society, it is apparent that democratic parenting cannot utilize autocratic methods. In an autocratic society, autocratic methods such as punishment will work effectively. But in a democratic society the use of democratic parenting principles will be the most effective. The exceptional child should not be excluded as society incorporates the concept of equality through the application of democratic principles in our parenting. If we make an *exception* for any child by not applying democratic principles, we run the risk of having that child feel out of place in our society. Belonging is the primary motivation for us all, and our children are *no exception* to the rule. If we do make an exception for our children who are handicapped or suffer from some other disability, then we act to compound the difficulties they may experience in finding a place in society.

2

DEVELOPMENT OF BEHAVIOR PATTERNS
IN CHILDREN

The Johnson family has three children: eleven-year-old Beth, nine-year-old James, and six-year-old Lois. The Millers also have three children. Mary, their youngest child, has polio. This factor considerably changes the perception Mary has about herself and the way the other children see her and treat her. Lois and Mary are both six years old and are both the youngest in their family. Yet, their perception of themselves and their behavior is different because of the physical problems Mary has encountered.

Each child needs to find a place in the world, and a child like Mary is greatly affected in her view of herself by the circumstances of being physically handicapped. A child's behavior is affected by his need to find his place. All his actions and behaviors are aimed at this goal.

Since children develop behavior patterns to reach an immediate goal, we can state that children's behavior is goal-directed. It does serve a purpose. It may be difficult to believe that our children's behavior is purposive, but even the most disruptive behaviors have a purpose. This concept of purposive behavior is true for *all* children, whether fully functioning or exceptional. Parents of exceptional children may have a harder time believing that their child's behavior has a purpose. But poor motor coordination or intellectual limitations do not interfere with a child wanting to develop a sense of belonging or in having purposive behavior. However, these factors do affect how she thinks she can find her place. Your child will not be able to tell you why she kicks the walls, for children are not consciously aware of their purpose. They simply observe their surroundings and use the behaviors that aid them in finding their place in the family. Children do not consciously calculate which behaviors have a payoff or which behaviors serve their purpose in gaining a sense of belonging. However, those behaviors that do not aid the child's efforts to belong—to win recognition on a regular, fairly predictable basis—are simply put aside and are not repeated.

We can better understand the purpose of a child's behaviors when we understand the factors that affect a child's perception of his world. Mary's perception of how she thinks she should act is greatly affected by how she thinks people see her. Having polio greatly affects how she believes people see her.

INNER ENVIRONMENT

We can call the things that a child brings with her into the world her *inner environment*. The child's inherited characteristics form her inner environment. These characteristics include such things as height, weight, intellectual ability, special talents, and so on. Billie Anderson, who is not as coordinated as other children, is made fun of by them. His inherited trait has an effect on him. Brad, who does not have the proper amount of growth hormone and has grown only an inch in two years, is influenced by his inherited traits. He sees people trying to help him because he is very small. They think he's cute! He now begins to discover that if he appears to have a hard time doing something, someone will come to his rescue. Being small has influenced his way of finding his place in the world.

Exceptional children are usually particularly influenced by inherited factors. Below-average intellectual skills or physical capacities create certain limitations in children, and thus people respond to them differently. It is how we respond to them that affects their perception of themselves. Brad isn't helpless, but because he experienced a necessity for others to provide "help" in training him, he has learned that he can get more service from others by being helpless. He is actually capable of doing many of the things that people do for him, but helplessness has become Brad's method for finding his place.

A handicap sets certain functional limits, but the child's perception of the handicap minimizes or maximizes his achievement of his potential. To increase the child's potential, parents need to be sensitive to these self-perceptions.

Betty, who has always been told how beautiful she is, is never able to relax. She feels that being pretty is the only way people will appreciate her. Thus she finds her place by being pretty. It is important that parents recognize that these inner environmental factors such as physical capacities and intellectual skills affect all children. It does not necessarily mean that because a child is physically impaired or intellectually handicapped that she will have a bad perception of herself. As with Betty, even the most positive traits may be interpreted negatively. Conversely, the most negative traits can also have positive effects on how a child finds his place.

Very often a child who experiences a particulaı handicap develops other skills and builds upon his strengths to overcompensate for the handicap. It is important for us to be aware that the handicap is not as important as the child's subjective interpretation of the handicap. It is our responsibility to see how our children are viewing their world and to assist them in constructively finding their place.

OUTER ENVIRONMENT

In addition to a child's inner environment, the child's *outer environment* influences the development of personality. The child's outer environment includes family atmosphere, family constellation, and parental child-rearing practices. All these factors affect the child's development and the manner in which he learns to deal with life's tasks.

Family Atmosphere

The *family atmosphere* is established by the parents. The family is the child's first encounter with a social group, and it becomes a model world for her first introduction to values, attitudes, and human relationships. Economic, ethnic, and religious values held by the parents will be communicated to the child and incorporated into her frame of reference. She will try to integrate these values and attitudes expressed by the parents in a manner that will allow her to gain a sense of belonging in the family.

Patricia, a six-year-old brain-damaged child, cannot be out of her mother's sight without screaming, crying, and becoming disruptive. One factor influencing her behavior is that her father feels she has to learn the cold facts of life the way he did, while her mother feels she needs almost total care.

Patricia senses her parents' different attitudes and capitalizes on the one parent's attitude to attain the total involvement of her mother.

A socially conscious parent spends a great deal of time preparing her severely retarded five-year-old son to look "cute" and say "hi" to people at church. Yet she spends almost no time at home enjoying the child. The attitude conveyed to any child greatly influences how the child responds. The child senses the attitude of the parents. Parents will also find that the child discovers what most upsets them. It would not be unusual for this child, who decides he wants his parents' attention, to start to act out in public. Past responses will have taught him that his parents respond more quickly because they are concerned about how others view them as parents. They are especially sensitive because they have an exceptional child.

If parents place a high value upon monetary goods, so may the child. The child's view of different ethnic groups will also often be in line with that expressed by the parents. If the parents feel they are better than others, then the child may develop feelings of superiority toward others and exhibit behaviors that try to maintain superior-inferior relationships with other individuals.

One cannot predict whether or not a child will adhere strongly to the beliefs and values of his parents. Each child observes and interprets the given surroundings and determines his views on how to find a place, or gain a sense of belonging and security. A child whose parents quarrel frequently, show little affection, and try to dominate each other has few opportunities to develop positive human relationships. However, such a child can rely upon her own inner strength and motivation to relate to individuals in a productive manner. Not all children who come from homes of low economic status with parents who may feel "the world owes us a living" will hold the same belief. While the family atmosphere and parental attitudes lend support for the adoption of similar views, the child's own creativity, motivation, and subjectivity may lead to very different views.

Sometimes the child's behavior is exactly the opposite of his attitude. The child who is very sloppy may actually wish to be well organized like his father. Yet, each time he makes a less than perfect attempt to be neat and organized, the father is critical. The child wants to be neat and organized, fears not being so, yet becomes more disorganized, to the dismay of both himself and his father. In this situation, parental criticism discourages the child's attempt to live up to parental expectations. Severe criticism by parents typically fosters behavior opposite to what the parents desire.

The family atmosphere that presents the child with her first introduction to values, attitudes, and role models will influence her manner of coping with life. Just how she will be influenced cannot be predetermined. A son who sees his father indulge heavily in alcohol may at an early age copy such behavior, believing this to be a proper manly trait. On the other hand, the son may abstain totally from alcohol, seeing only negative outcomes from its use. A daughter whose parents constantly argue and whose mother dominates and controls the father may develop the belief that "women need to maintain dominance over men." The opposite view might also be adopted in this case! The daughter may develop a passive style, believing that this will alleviate all future difficulties with men and create a perfect, harmonious relationship. The influence of the family atmosphere is clear, but the direction and exact impact of this influence depend on the child's interpretation of the situation.

Family Constellation

The *family constellation* involves the positioning of children in relation to one another. John is the firstborn. His parents find pride and joy in everything he does. John is the first to crawl, the first to sit up, and the first to walk. John has been able to find his place through achievement, which comes fairly easily, since John is the only child and there is no imposing threat of competition. What happens, though, when John is two years old and a new baby is brought into the family?

John is no longer an only child; he no longer finds ease in capturing his parents' undivided attention. The new baby, Suellen, now requires much attention from her parents. There are many basic needs to which the parents must attend. This time used to be devoted only to John. How does John deal with the feeling of losing his position? John's observations of the situation are correct—he no longer has his parents' individual attention—but John, like all children, easily misinterprets his observations. John is no less loved by his parents than before. Suellen simply requires much of her parents' time and attention.

There are many options open to John as he strives to maintain a place in the family. John may notice that through misbehavior—refusing to eat dinner or making a fuss at bedtime—he is able to command his parents' attention once again. He may even regress to performing the behaviors and actions of a baby. "It seems to work for Suellen, why not for me?" *Children would prefer to receive negative attention than no attention at all.* Negative and positive attention both fall under the heading of RECOGNITION. John's parents could bring him into the picture by having him help with the care of Suellen. By assisting in her care John may begin to realize that he can find his place in the family through constructive and useful behaviors. He may realize that he has skills and accomplishments that are different from Suellen's, and he can continue to develop useful behaviors.

Children are keen observers of their surroundings but easily misinterpret their observations and draw mistaken conclusions. John began to interpret the loss of his parents' attention as a loss of love. He needed to take action during this threatening time. He interpreted the arrival of a new family member as a threat. The importance of this situation lies with John's interpretation. It was not the importance of a new baby coming into the family but how he decided to deal with it.

A third child, Jane, now comes into the family, taking over the place of the youngest. John does not feel as threatened as he previously did, since his competencies and achievements are so much more advanced than the youngest. However, Suellen loses her position as the youngest and now becomes the middle child. She also has decisions to make on how she will maintain her position in the family, as John did upon her arrival. No child enters the family with the same family constellation. With the addition of each family member, the family constellation, the positioning of the children, changes.

John, who is the oldest child, may strive to maintain his position as the first and becomes the "pace setter." Suellen may try to catch up and surpass John in his achievements, causing John to decide to give up and feel as though it is too difficult to maintain his number-one spot. Suellen, on the other hand, may decide that John is too advanced in his skills and may choose to take on other areas of interest. John is an A student in his academic work, so Suellen develops a distaste for academics and becomes interested in music. The youngest child, Jane, may find her place not through accomplishments, but rather through control. By becoming the helpless "baby," Jane places others in her service. She "needs" someone to lend assistance. This gives her control.

The exceptional child is greatly influenced by the family constellation. Allen, who is the oldest in his family, has a severe case of arthritis. He is limited in the degree to which he can pursue many rigorous activities, such as sports. Duane, his younger brother, always competes with Allen's special treatment. He tries "extra hard" to attain recognition as "the athlete" as a means of competing with Allen. This situation can be dangerous to both Allen and to Duane. Allen can get the feeling of not being OK because he can't play sports, and Duane can feel that he always needs to get recognition to feel that he is special. We, as parents, must be aware that this competitiveness exists in every family and among all children. Families with handicapped children are no exception.

All children in the family have an influence upon one another. Eventually each will discover how he can maintain his place and keep the others in their place. It is the influence between the children that will have the greatest effect upon how the siblings develop their unique place in the family structure. The possibilities that can develop are as numerous as there are children.

The parents of Bob, a trainable retarded sixteen-year-old boy, cannot understand why he is so outgoing and enjoys pleasing people. Bob is very different from his trainable retarded fourteen-year-old sister, Jean. Bob gets recognition from his parents for how he acts around people. Jean, on the other hand, doesn't feel she is as good as Bob in being able to please others and relate socially; therefore, she becomes more withdrawn. Bob and Jean influence how they see each other, and eventually each finds his place.

The children in the family will influence one another, each one choosing a particular course of action. Whatever the action might be, its purpose is to find a significant place in the family. The "tomboy," the "monster," the "baby," and the "helpless" are all possibilities for children. Each child will determine her course of action by how she interprets her position in the family. Again, the interpretation is more important than the actual position. Not all eldest children will develop the same characteristics or use the same manner to secure their place. Not all children with the same learning disability or handicap will view it in the same light. Each child in his own unique manner will develop a goal, a highly individualized approach to achieve a feeling of significance and belonging.

Child-Rearing Methods

The third and final factor in the child's outer environment is the *child-rearing methods* used by the parents. A constant interaction occurs between a child and her parents. The child quickly learns that mother and father have particular reactions to particular behaviors. A child who has lost the power of speech may have parents who react with guilt and pity. She senses this reaction and may adopt a similar attitude of self-pity and allow herself to become helpless. She may also choose not to accept her parents' reaction, and instead of giving up, she may face the handicap with courage and deal with it the best way she can.

Susie, a child with a learning disability, does poorly in school, although she has special classes and assistance. Her parents pose an even greater obstacle. They are embarrassed that their daughter cannot keep up with the rest of the children. Having to deal with her learning disability is now compounded by having to deal with her parents' discouragement. Susie could easily quit trying in school, since her parents offer little support. However, she does not give up but maintains her efforts and strives toward fulfilling her potential.

Children learn to maintain certain behaviors for their payoff. The reaction to a child's behavior may accidentally reinforce unwanted behaviors. Seven-year-old Jimmy is an only child who suffered considerable brain damage. Jimmy's parents became cautious of his actions. One day Jimmy hit his head in disgust while trying to put a puzzle together. His parents' reactions were strong and immediate. "Stop that! Don't do that!" Within three days Jimmy needed a helmet to protect him because he was banging his head so much. Every time he hit his head, they would hold him and try to stop him. He discovered that his behavior got mom and dad's total attention. Their reaction to his head banging actually continued the behavior rather than diminishing it, as they had hoped.

The child does something accidentally, the parents react to it, the child interprets the reaction and chooses to keep or discard the behavior. Exceptional children may exhibit certain behavior as a result of the specific handicap or disability. These behaviors are no different from those of the average child in that the exceptional child may choose to increase or control the behavior according to the payoff received. Among *all* children behavior can either be reinforced or diminished by the parents' reaction. The difference with exceptional children is the degree to which they may be able to control certain behaviors.

The child's decisions in how he will achieve significance, a place in the family, are influenced by the child's inherited qualities, both physical and intellectual; the child's family atmosphere, which introduces values and attitudes; the child's family constellation, which aids in development of self-concept, and the child-rearing methods, which lend guidance to the child. The child takes all these factors into consideration in developing his approach to life. The child devises a life plan, based on his interpretations, that he believes will lead toward his basic goal of finding a place. This life plan is well developed by about age five. It is not foolproof, since it is based upon his interpretations, which are not always accurate.

As the child grows and encounters more and more social situations, she begins to incorporate new behaviors and modify old ones in accordance with her life plan. Her views and ideas on how to find her place have not changed. The external behaviors are strictly adjustments to new external situations. These new behaviors are merely alternate methods of reaching the child's previously established goal. Therefore, if we understand her life plan, new behaviors will not be confusing to us. Her goal remains the same. Johnny can receive attention in many different ways: Fighting brings his parents on the run. Needing special assistance to eat brings one kind of attention, and helping to clean the house brings another kind of attention. A child will utilize all powers of creativity and ingenuity to achieve his goal.

3

CHARACTERISTICS OF
EXCEPTIONAL CHILDREN

This entire book deals with children's misbehavior and ways to eliminate certain annoying behaviors they adopt. However, in dealing with misbehavior of exceptional children, there is another factor that needs to be taken into consideration: the actual effect of a physical or mental handicap. Parents who do not have exceptional children may not understand that there are certain behavioral characteristics associated with certain dysfunctions in children. If we do not understand these natural behaviors they may begin to appear as misbehavior, or they may accentuate an existing misbehavior.

Valerie, age twelve, was retarded but educable. Her mother reported very few behavioral problems. But one difficulty was frustrating, confusing, and costly to mother: Valerie would constantly pick at her clothes, especially those made of double-knit fabrics and the panty hose that she liked to wear. It became a daily routine of mother yelling at Valerie for destroying her clothes. Valerie would find a thread and pull on it; within minutes there were numerous pulls all over her clothing. She appeared to have an uncontrollable need to find every loose thread and pull on it. This had the effect of virtually destroying much of her clothing.

Did Valerie have an uncontrollable urge to pick at her clothing? It is understandable that mother was confused in trying to understand her daughter's behavior.

Here is a situation that often occurs with parents of exceptional children. The mother was unaware that her daughter was exhibiting an attention-getting behavior to which she responded. Valerie exhibited a characteristic often associated with developmentally disabled children. This characteristic is commonly known as *perseveration* and involves automatic continuation of behavior that the child has great difficulty controlling. In Valerie's case, picking at her clothes was not uncontrollable. However, it was accentuated by her perseveration. Her mother could control this behavior by utilizing systematic remedial procedures and allowing more time for Valerie to develop internal control.

In Valerie's situation we have a characteristic of perseveration that occurs naturally and exaggerates a simple attention-getting behavior. When perseveration and the misbehavior are combined, a more complex difficulty develops for the parent to remedy. It is understandable that Valerie's mother was confused and frustrated. She did not understand why her daughter would continue to pull her clothes, since she really liked to wear those clothes. In attempting to diminish the thread pulling, mother did not take into consideration the effect perseveration had on this misbehavior. Once she understood this, it became clear to her why Valerie didn't respond to her corrective measures, and she was able to deal with Valerie's misbehavior more effectively. Mother now knows that it may naturally take longer to remedy the difficulty because of her child's disability.

The remedy needed was for Valerie to gain a sense of control over her behavior. It was recommended to mother, after she understood the goal of attention getting, that she develop a systematic procedure for combating this difficulty. A logical consequence (see chapter 9) was devised to help diminish the misbehavior. Valerie was told that if she was able to control pulling threads on her clothes, she would be able to continue to wear her nice double-knit fabrics. It was further explained to Valerie that if she was unable to control pulling the threads she would have to wear other fabrics. This was implemented with an initial two-day period of wearing other fabrics, after which Valerie would be allowed to wear her favorite double-knit clothing. If the pulling continued, double-knit clothing was removed for three days. The procedure was systematically continued with increasing lengths of time. In this way Valerie began to learn to combat the effects of her perseveration by developing more internal control over her behavior.

The point is that characteristics such as perseveration in developmentally disabled children will occur naturally as part of the disability. Parents need to take this into consideration in establishing realistic goals for modifying their children's misbehavior. Without this understanding of the relationships between the particular characteristics of the disability and the misbehavior, parents may actually accentuate a child's misbehavior.

This situation with Valerie illustrates that before they take corrective procedures, parents need to know how the disability may or may not be affecting the child's misbehavior. In Valerie's case, the perseveration affected the initial attention-getting behavior of thread pulling, prolonging the time needed to diminish this misbehavior. But when this was understood, the task of redirecting Valerie's behavior became easier. The misbehavior of exceptional children and the characteristics of their disability may adversely reinforce each other. If they do not take this relationship into consideration, parents may assume that their child's misbehavior is purely an outgrowth of the disability, believing there is very little that could be done to remedy it. This is not to say that all misbehavior is solely a function of a child seeking a mistaken goal that is correctable by the parents, but that there may be a relationship between the behaviors caused by a disability and the behavior resulting from a child's pursuit of a mistaken goal. Behaviors that occur in exceptional children may be significantly interrelated and greatly affect one another.

To avoid any confusion, we need to follow the steps Valerie's mother followed.

Step 1: Upon observing a misbehavior, analyze the mistaken goal exhibited (see chapter 7). (Valerie: Attention getting—mistaken goal 1)

Step 2: Know the characteristics that occur naturally in your child's specific disability. (Valerie: Developmental disability—perseveration)

Step 3: Analyze characteristics from step 2 that might adversely affect the misbehavior observed in step 1. (Valerie: Perseveration perpetuated initial attention-getting behavior)

Step 4: Establish corrective procedures based upon your findings in step 3. (Valerie: Logical consequences plus a longer period of time systematically implemented)

The four-step procedure should also be used in the situation below.

Scott was a dyslexic child who exhibited the characteristics of low attention span. His parents did not understand that many learning-disabled children exhibit low attention spans. Because of their lack of understanding they consistently reprimanded Scott for his low attention span and easy distractability; they felt Scott was lazy and was not applying himself. A major power struggle developed between Scott and his parents. Due to their lack of understanding of the characteristics affecting learning-disabled children, they actually developed Scott's disability into a misbehavior. Once they understood the relationship between the disability and his misbehavior, the parents avoided entering into power struggles and began developing more positive approaches to Scott's low attention span.

Consultation with experts or qualified organizations (see appendix 3) knowledgeable in your child's disability may be beneficial. As you become more knowledgeable about your child's disability, it will become easier for you to establish specific remedial procedures through application of the four-step process just discussed. You will develop the most effective parenting procedures by combining your knowledge of the child's misbehavior with an awareness of the characteristics often associated with your child's disability.

4

COMMON BEHAVIOR PATTERNS
OF EXCEPTIONAL CHILDREN

Larry is a fourth grader from a middle-class neighborhood. His first two years in school were uneventful. When he reached the third grade, he began to exhibit some major reading problems. Upon diagnosis of the difficulty, Larry was assigned special tutoring three times a week to overcome it. Progress was extremely slow. The teacher spent more time with Larry but found that gains made were not retained between sessions. Both Larry and the teacher became frustrated. After a while the teacher reversed her approach and lessened the amount of responsibility she took for helping Larry to read. Although no immediate progress was made, after a few weeks definite improvement began to be evident. By the end of the year Larry was overcoming many of his reading difficulties.

Why do you think the teacher made greater progress after she reversed her approach in tutoring? One would expect that the more energy she put into assisting Larry with his reading difficulties, the greater the progress would be. However, this was not the case. The teacher discovered that Larry had numerous problems related to reading, but she also discovered that the more time and attention she spent with him individually, the more problems and difficulties he exhibited. Larry discovered more quickly than the teacher that he got more attention for what he didn't know than for what he did know.

The difficult task for the teacher was to provide special assistance in a manner that would not promote Larry's attention-getting behaviors.

PAMPEREDNESS

Many children who need special assistance like Larry exhibit characteristics similar to those of pampered, or spoiled, children. This pamperedness is a typical behavior pattern likely to develop in exceptional children. As with Larry, attention-getting behaviors become an easy route to receive pampering. These characteristics develop because we as parents provide special assistance that we believe will improve certain abilities in our children and help them overcome their problems. However, children interpret much of this special help as positive recognition. Although they may not like going to the reading specialist, physical therapist, hearing clinic, or speech therapist, they none-theless quickly learn that their disability provides them with much service and attention. This service and attention then comes to be demanded in the same way it is by spoiled children. The misinterpretation of this special assistance can cause children to believe, "This is the way life is, always having people in my service, doing things for me." Larry, like other children, does not understand that the attention given to him is to help him overcome certain problems. Doesn't it make sense that with all these people doing things for Larry that he would begin to expect and demand the attention?

Pamperedness is often a natural outgrowth from the special assistance we must provide our children. Although it is a natural occurrence, we can offset some of the effects by changing the way we give assistance.

Pamperedness can take many forms and can be exhibited in many ways.

Ann, at four years of age, fell, injured her head, and began to receive intense medical care. She lost all sense of balance and needed to be totally retrained in eating, toilet training, walking, and other basic skills. Mother spent tremen-dous amounts of time during a two-year period helping her down steps, making sure she didn't fall, and retraining her to eat. One day mother was outside talking to a neighbor and not paying much attention to Ann. Ann began screaming and crying, demanding that her mother return to the house. Ann's mother now found that she could not leave her daughter's sight.

Temper tantrums like those of Ann's are nothing more than an effective means of attempting to control parents' behavior. Through the process of regaining her skills, Ann developed the belief, "I should have the service of my mother at all times, and whatever I want I should get." Because of mother's total involvement with her, there was no need for Ann to demand anything—mother was always there. When things began to change and Ann was not getting mother's total involvement, she used whatever means were available to regain the total involvement of her mother.

Temper tantrums are typical behaviors exhibited by children. Because our exceptional children get so much of our and other people's time, they exhibit the same characteristics as pampered children. It may sound inappropriate to talk about exceptional children as being pampered, but the characteristic belief that "everything revolves around me" is the same in many exceptional children as in many spoiled children.

Another way children can interpret our special assistance can be shown through the behavior of Leon.

Leon is a seven-year-old trainable retarded child. He entered first grade with few self-help skills such as dressing or feeding himself. A great deal of effort was made to teach Leon these basic skills. By the end of the school year, Leon became quite good at buttoning his shirts and feeding himself. However, during the summer, while he was away from school, Leon discovered that any frustration exhibited was almost immediately relieved by his parents. Because he did spill some food, his parents slowly began to help him to eat. By the end of the summer Leon could no longer eat by himself or dress himself. The school staff was surprised that Leon had regressed and had no more skills than when he'd entered first grade.

Leon was incapable of remembering what he had learned in school because he was not given the opportunity to practice the skills at home. He found it easier for someone else to do it for him than to go through the frustration of learning. Leon's parents, in an attempt to lessen his frustration, taught him that it was not necessary to become self-sufficient because there were so many people to do things for him.

In the foregoing examples we find that some children, like Larry, believe they can get *attention* from others for their lack of performance. Others, like Ann, who have so many things done for them, learn that they can do just as they please by *demanding* service from others. On the other hand, Leon found that people would do things for him if he simply appeared *helpless* to do for himself or became too frustrated at trying. All three forms of behavior are exhibited in varying degrees by the pampered child.

Because we need to provide our children with necessary assistance to learn various skills, we run the risk of developing a behavior pattern similar to that of spoiled children. Consequently we must develop techniques to redirect their misperception of the assistance we provide them.

DISCOURAGEMENT

The second major behavior pattern present in many handicapped children is that of *discouragement,* created by the feeling that they are incapable, that there is "something wrong" with them. The numerous failures that our children experience lead them to believe that they cannot possibly accomplish any task they attempt.

Ed has gone through five years in school without having anyone realize that he has a hearing loss in his left ear. He is intelligent, yet has received average to slightly below average grades. In a new open classroom Ed began to experience more consistent failures in school. His grades dropped and he became more confused about his assignments. As a result of this, Ed refused to go to school, crying at home in the mornings and eventually attempting to destroy his school books.

The numerous failures that Ed experienced in a less structured environment resulted in his feeling that he was "dumb" and in his hating school. His misbehavior at home was his attempt to avoid going back to school and facing continuous failures. He saw the other children being treated differently, and he began to feel separate from the group. This sense of being different and of not belonging created an overall feeling of not being OK.

The potential discouragement of our children who are in some way handicapped is a reality we must all face. We live in a society where value is placed upon success and perfection. When we live with the idea that winning is not only the most important thing, but the only thing, the potential for discouragement in exceptional children is almost inevitable.

OVERCOMPENSATION

Overcompensation is the third major behavior pattern exhibited by exceptional children. The behavior pattern can result in positive or negative outcomes. A child who has orthopedic problems may desire to be on the track team. Instead of adjusting to the type of athletic activity he can do, he totally avoids athletics and puts all of his energy into becoming an academic success. Although his becoming a success in the area of academics may be a positive effort, this child negatively avoids the area of athletics because he cannot be successful as a track star.

This type of compensation would become more obvious if it were directed toward negative behaviors. Another child with orthopedic problems may avoid all athletic activities and direct her energies in becoming more critical of others involved in various forms of athletics. In both cases, the child compensates for a handicap but avoids altogether her desired area of interest. Being handicapped in a certain area of activity does not necessitate the avoidance of that particular area. It does entail the adjustment to certain physical realities. Again, the same child may not be able to become a track star, but she can attend track meets, become an announcer at track meets, or participate in various other aspects of track.

Pamperedness, discouragement, and overcompensation are not evident in all children. Yet, they do exist in some form or another in all exceptional children. As parents, our awareness of these behavior patterns is vital in establishing the initial step for the redirection of our children's misperceptions and unconstructive behaviors.

5

CHARACTERISTICS OF
THE EXCEPTIONAL PARENT

Susanne is a trainable retarded five-year-old enrolled in a special kindergarten program offered in the local school district. This program is designed for children with intellectual handicaps to enrich their skill level before they enter the first grade. Susanne exhibited deficiencies in speech and self-care skills. Most of Susanne's classmates of the same age had slightly less developed skills. The special kindergarten program allowed Susanne to progress and increase her self-care skills and speech ability throughout the year. Susanne's parents viewed this progress as enormous. Compared with the other children, she appeared to be far superior in intellectual abilities. When it came time for Susanne's parents to enroll her in the special first-grade class for trainable and severely retarded children, a natural follow-up to the special kindergarten program, Susanne's parents refused. The teachers were surprised about the parents' refusal and later found out that the parents were attempting to enroll Susanne in a regular first-grade class. Because of Susanne's superiority over her classmates, her parents felt that she was capable of performing regular classroom work.

What made Susanne's parents take this new course of action? They know that Susanne is a trainable retarded child and needs special assistance. Susanne's parents reacted in a very typical fashion.

26

Most parents want to be "good parents." They want to make sure their children receive every possible opportunity and advantage to be successful. If the child does well, the parents have done a good job; if the child does poorly, the parents have done a poor job. Like so many other parents, Susanne's parents wanted her to achieve and be successful in spite of her given limitations. They wanted Susanne to succeed so they could feel that they had been "good parents." The need to be a "good parent" is common among all parents. Parents of exceptional children sometimes exaggerate this need because of the apparent limitations of the child.

In addition to this need to be "good parents," parents must learn to cope with their own emotional response to having an exceptional child. The need of Susanne's parents to be good parents, combined with the emotional reaction of denying Susanne's need for special assistance in school, was leading to her enrollment in a regular first-grade class. Susanne's parents felt this to be the best course of action, but they were denying the basic limitations exhibited by their daughter. This is commonly known as the "good parent syndrome." Parents often try so hard to provide for their child that they stifle them. Susanne's parents, like other parents of exceptional children, have a need for their children to succeed. Susanne's parents misinterpreted the progress she had made in the special kindergarten program to mean that she had overcome her basic limitations. The need for success and the need to be good parents make the emotional reaction of denial a common response to a child's handicap. Many such parents cannot fulfill their own needs to be "good parents" if they realistically face the limitations of their children.

By denying certain realities Susanne's parents may hinder their daughter's true potential. Coping with their own feelings of having an exceptional child is crucial. Emotional reactions that accompany being a parent of an exceptional child must be recognized and dealt with appropriately. Susanne's parents did not deal with their feelings of denial, causing them to put tremendous amounts of energy into unrealistic goals. We can direct our energies toward encouraging independence in our children only by dealing appropriately with our emotional reactions.

Denial is only one of the numerous emotional responses parents exhibit. Reactions can take many forms. For example, the mother who has a child with cerebral palsy asks God, "What did I do to deserve this?" The mother reacts with feelings of *bitterness* when she recognizes the additional care and responsibilities that will have to be taken on. This bitterness can be directed toward the child, society, or individuals who are working with the family. Parents may attack and criticize physical therapists, special-education teachers, and physicians, trying to transfer "the blame" from themselves. The nonacceptance of exceptional children by society in general fosters this parental reaction, and it is typical for parents to direct this feeling toward the child or toward each other.

A mother was angered at a school official for removing her trainable retarded daughter from the lunchroom after she threw her food on the floor. More than anger is being expressed by this parent—she is consistently angry with anyone who uses corrective measures with her daughter. Why is the mother angry when her child is receiving realistic treatment? She has never taken any corrective action for fear of losing her daughter's love. When others take steps to correct the child, mother believes they are putting extra burdens on the child, not understanding her child's problems. The *anger* is mother's way of protecting her daughter. In actuality she is *over*protecting her.

Rejection is another common emotional reaction of parents. Parents who find it difficult to spend any necessary extra time with their exceptional child may appear to be rejecting them. What may to all outward appearances seem to be rejection is sometimes really an expression of the parents' inability to cope with their child. The parents are actually experiencing a sense of helplessness.

Sam is an excited expectant father who anticipates a son to carry on the family name. Upon being told that his wife gave birth to a mongoloid son, Sam reacts with deep feelings of grief. Sam is depressed. He cries. He can't sleep or eat.

The feelings of *mourning* or *grief* that Sam experiences are similar to those experienced by someone who has lost a loved one. In Sam's mind, he has lost a loved one. He lost the perfect son for which he had hoped. For a time Sam withdraws from the world and sits around day and night as if in mourning.

Another feeling that tends to be extremely common among parents of exceptional children is that of *guilt*. Typical statements by parents that are often related to feelings of guilt are: "I could have prevented this if only . . .," "Why did I bring the child into the world?" "I'm not doing enough—I should be doing more," "People just don't understand the help they need," "I must have done something wrong to have this happen to me," and "How can I enjoy myself when my child has to suffer?" In most cases statements such as these are unproductive. They merely serve in the development and continuation of guilt feelings. Feelings of guilt may be extremely typical, but they stand in the way of the child's progress. Maintaining guilt feelings takes energy that could be directed toward more productive and useful behavior.

The realities are that parents of exceptional children are likely to experience many of these emotional reactions. Although these feelings are natural and are to be expected, they are usually unproductive and greatly detract from the parents' ability to be good parents in the true sense. Only when the parents become aware of and acknowledge these feelings and thereby come to deal with them realistically do they give their child the opportunity to fullfill his potential, and only then will the parents become comfortable with themselves in dealing with their child. The longer parents hold on to these feelings, the less chance their children have to reach their fullest potential. No one is saying that it is easy to deal with having an exceptional child, but parents can choose to make the situation harder or easier.

6

THE EXCEPTIONAL CHILD:
The Effects on Other Children

When most people think of a family with an exceptional child, they fail to realize the impact of that child on the family structure. The Halls were confronted with such a situation. They had two children before Cathy came along. Cathy has cerebral palsy and initially needed special assistance from her parents. The Halls had another child two years later. If you were to ask Cathy's mother what she thought was the most difficult part of coping with her children, you'd think she would say Cathy, right? But in the Hall family, like in many others, the main difficulty may surround the other children in the family.

As stated earlier, two of the components that have a great effect upon personality development are the family constellation and the child's inherited qualities. It is not difficult to see that an exceptional child greatly affects how the other children see themselves in the family.

ATTENTION GETTING

The exceptional child's effect can take many forms.

The Levensons have four children at home, one of whom is a trainable retarded nine-year-old girl. The special assistance Carolyn receives has had a

30

profound effect upon the other children's view of themselves. One of Mr. Levenson's main complaints is that the children cannot play as a group without fighting. The other children noticed that Carolyn was receiving a lot of special attention, and they wanted this special attention also. They became disruptive when it came to sharing as a family because there was no specialness related to being cooperative. They discovered that the more trouble they caused, the more undivided attention they each received. When they couldn't get along, mom and dad would take time out to play a "special game" just with each of them. All the children engaged in some type of attention getting. One child became the "good kid," doing all the right things to get praise from others. One couldn't get to sleep unless she had all her toys and a special story read to her at night. Another developed reading problems, requiring tutoring by a specialist and by mom and dad. Each child developed behaviors designed to elicit more and more individual attention from mom and dad, who were always exhausted from trying to meet all their children's "special" needs.

The Levenson children are not unique because they want attention. The behaviors they exhibit began because they felt Carolyn was getting too much help, and they wanted it as well. So much of mom and dad's time is spent trying to deal with the other children's special needs that the house is usually in total chaos. Carolyn's parents don't understand that the more they play individual games with the children, the more the children will demand attention. The children learn they do not have to work together, that in fact working together cooperatively gets them less rather than more of what they want—mom and dad's attention.

RESENTMENT

The Levenson children respond to the exceptional child in their family by competing for special attention through unconstructive means. Not all siblings respond in this manner. Often the other children see how much attention is devoted to the exceptional child and tend to deal with this in a resentful manner, rejecting the exceptional sibling. This resentment is often exhibited through negative acts, such as hitting the exceptional child or blaming something on him. The other children feel that the exceptional child is the cause of their not receiving the involvement from their parents that they feel they deserve. They resent him for receiving large amounts of special attention. The other siblings may interpret the attention given to the exceptional child as proof that they are being rejected by the parents because, "if they really loved me, they would want to spend more time with me."

Other facets of the resentment may be an attempt by siblings to make the exceptional child look bad, thereby making themselves look good to receive more attention from their parents.

Dad spent two weeks organizing all his receipts and preparing the tax return. One afternoon the older brother observed his handicapped brother beginning to get into their father's tax material on the desk. Rather than removing him from the room or getting someone to help, the brother purposely let it happen. He let his father know that he saw his younger brother mess up the father's work. This not only made his younger brother look bad, but also made him look good and allowed him to get more positive involvement from the parents.

Families with exceptional children are open to these types of situations. They occur not because the parents are doing things wrong but because of the family structure. The other children may perceive many inequalities in terms of time and involvement from parents, creating a highly competitive relationship among siblings for attention.

PROTECTIVENESS

Claude's sister Colleen, who was born with a cleft palate, was made fun of by the neighborhood children. Claude was constantly in fights with other children over Colleen. When children made fun of Colleen, Claude would come to her defense. He became extremely protective toward and highly sensitive about his sister.

Siblings of an exceptional child may develop a highly protective role. This may include fighting to protect the exceptional child and excessive worrying about him. It is also not uncommon for other siblings to take on the role of the "super parent" as a means of finding their place in the family. They desire no time for themselves and appear to devote all their energy toward meeting the needs of the exceptional child. It may even get to the point where a child is almost literally a martyr, giving up her own life to take care of the exceptional sibling. We as parents need to be cautious lest the conscientious helper give up everything, including her own identity, to help the exceptional child. Children need to have a sense of responsibility toward one another, but when this is taken to an extreme, the parents need to assist the children to be more realistic in offering their help and in the manner they use to find their place in the family.

OVERCOMPENSATION

As explained previously, the major motivator of behavior in a child is his desire to find his place in the family. In families with an exceptional child, the emphasis is often on overcoming various types of deficiencies and handicaps. Because of this emphasis the other children begin to feel that they are not able to get as much recognition as they feel they deserve by performing their activities in an average way. This may generate the feeling that they need to exaggerate their skills, or overcompensate. The family whose child has a learning disability may find another sibling attempting to excel in that same area in school or academic work.

Overcompensation is not necessarily detrimental to the individual, but it can become damaging if it's carried to the extreme, when the individual begins to believe that she is only worthwhile if she excels. If she does not get the highest grade possible, she may feel she is a failure. Because of the extreme feeling generated by her attempt to overcompensate, it seems that nothing short of academic perfection is acceptable. Even though the child may have done her best, she does not feel successful because of her overreaction to the deficiencies of her exceptional sibling.

A more unproductive form of overcompensation is demonstrated by Jonathan, whose older brother, Jimmy, is a hemophiliac. Since Jimmy leads a somewhat more restricted life, not engaging in activities that entail a risk of injury, Jonathan has become more of a risk taker. He engages in rugged and physically hazardous activities in which Jimmy can in no way participate. Jonathan's overcompensation holds the potential of personal injury to himself and therefore is an unproductive method of finding his place.

IMITATION

One of the most frustrating ways in which some siblings act to gain recognition is the imitation of the undesirable behaviors exhibited by the exceptional child. The other children observe the particular reaction or attention given by the parents for negative behaviors of an exceptional child and imitate these negative behaviors to receive more recognition from the parents. Children view any parental involvement, positive or negative, as equally important, so it is easy to understand why the other children would imitate negative behavior. They see the recognition and involvement it gets the exceptional child.

Molly's parents as well as the neighbors became quite upset when they noticed she openly relieved herself on the front lawn. This, of course, created emotional reactions in everybody. A few days later mother was even more astonished to see that one of her other children imitated Molly's behavior. Mother could not understand why he would even think of such a thing, since he was older and knew better.

Children imitate the behavior of others because they see the level of involvement that results from the behavior, in this case as a result of Molly's misbehavior. Children are not concerned with the severity of the misbehavior. The amount of attention outweighs any sense of right or wrong. Thus, all these behaviors, whether positive or negative, are purposeful. Children learn that certain behaviors create certain parental responses and learn how they can create that parental response.

Parents need to be aware of the many potential behavior patterns developed by the siblings of an exceptional child. The critical factor in understanding the development of behavior patterns relates to the primary motivator of all behavior—finding one's place. An exceptional child demands more involvement from the parents, which greatly affects how the other siblings find their place in the family. Parents' awareness of these family dynamics prepares them for many of these reactions: resentment, overcompensation, imitation of negative behaviors, etc. The feeling of not being able to get as much attention as the exceptional child is a typical family dynamic. These reactions can be either overcome or prevented by following many of the basic child-rearing practices to be discussed in the following chapters.

Basic Principles in Dealing with Exceptional Children

7

THE PURPOSE OF MISBEHAVIOR

One of the most crucial concepts that we need to understand is that children's misbehavior is purposeful. It is no accident that children consistently exhibit the same misbehavior. A child incorporates certain behaviors, both positive and negative, because she feels the behaviors will secure her place in the group. Often a child exhibits so many different misbehaviors that her parents find it difficult, if not impossible, to understand her goals. The following situations will show how children's misbehavior does serve a specific purpose.

Tommy, age ten, a trainable retarded child, constantly changes the television channels when his twelve-year-old brother Billy and his nine-year-old sister Mary are watching. Billy and Mary begin to yell at Tommy, "Get away and leave us alone." Mother hears the yelling from another room and comes to see what is happening. She sees Tommy being picked on by his brother and sister and tells the children to stop yelling at him. She walks over and gives Tommy a big hug and sits him on the couch. The bickering quiets down, but as soon as mother leaves the room, Tommy starts changing the channels and the battle flares up again. This time mother comes in and yells at Tommy's brother and sister, "Both of you should know better than to treat Tommy this way," and then proceeds to take Tommy with her into the other room.

When exceptional children misbehave, the parents assume they can't help themselves and that the misbehavior is to be expected because of the disability. As previously pointed out, some particular behavior disorders are inevitably associated with certain disabilities or handicaps. However, such behavior may become exaggerated and thus become a misbehavior. Also, exceptional children do often exhibit misbehavior totally unrelated to their disability.

MISTAKEN GOALS

Previously, the concept of belonging and children's desire to find their place in their group was stated as the major motivating factor of behavior. All behavior is purposive. Productive behavior as well as misbehavior can serve children in attaining an immediate goal.

Undue Attention

We term the goals that children seek to achieve by misbehavior *mistaken goals.*

There are four mistaken goals that explain the misbehavior of exceptional children. It is crucial that we become aware of the purpose of our children's misbehavior and become aware of the fact that misbehavior among exceptional children is purposive. It is awareness and knowledge that will allow us to provide effective guidance for our children.

Tommy has found that by creating a disturbance, he can command his mother's attention. Tommy is communicating the following belief through his misbehavior: "I only have a place when I get constant attention. When I'm not noticed, I don't belong." Tommy's misbehavior illustrates the first mistaken goal of children's misbehavior—*undue attention.*

There are two key factors in understanding attention-getting behavior. If we look at *mother's reaction,* the first factor, we notice that she was quick to respond. Her involvement was immediate, and her attention was given to Tommy as well as to the other children. Finally, mother gave her undivided attention to Tommy when she took him with her into another room. What more could Tommy ask? His annoying behavior got the recognition he was seeking. The *emotional feelings* that parents experience in response to their children's misbehavior is the second factor. When parents experience feelings of annoyance, frustration, or irritation, it indicates that the misbehavior is for the purpose of seeking attention.

Exceptional children are extremely sensitive to their surroundings and to parental reactions. Children will quickly adjust their behavior, incorporating new tactics and discarding old ones, to utilize the most effective behavior for reaching their goal. If the goal is attention, children can turn to the most useful or the most useless types of behavior. They can become cooperative or disruptive, depending on how they view the attention they receive. Usually parents don't question children who exhibit cooperative behavior. But why would children misbehave if they were scolded and punished as a result? The answer is simple. A child would rather be spanked than not be noticed at all. Whenever we react to a child's misbehavior and feed into his demands for attention, we only serve to reinforce his mistaken goal and belief that "I only count when I'm noticed."

Parents of exceptional children may experience difficulty in detecting what is misbehavior. Since exceptional children typically require special assistance in some area or another, there is an added difficulty in determining attention-getting behavior. The special assistance provided to exceptional children establishes situations that can easily encourage children to demand more and more attention. We need to step back from the situation and examine whether or not our children are requesting appropriate attention or demanding undue service. We also need to be consciously aware of whether or not a particular behavior is consistent. Very often children will show an inappropriate behavior only once. This is not a misbehavior that requires corrective measures. If a child spills a drink or soils her clothes once, it is not a misbehavior. An accident is an accident, and we must accept the fact that we all have accidents. Perfection is not part of being human.

Power

It was time for nine-year-old David, a trainable retarded child, to take his bath before bedtime. David doesn't particularly care to take baths and began to run around the house having mother pursue him in a chase. David would lock himself in one room after another, while mother grew more and more angry trying to capture him. Mother eventually gave up. She realized she could in no way overpower David. Since David usually had a snack after his bath before he went to bed, mother told him, "Since you're not going to take your bath, then you'll have to go straight to bed."

David was aware of his bedtime routine but decided to see who was the more powerful, mother or himself. By initiating a chase around the house and refusing to give in to his mother, David showed his ability to be powerful. Mother could have succumbed totally to David's power play if she allowed him to have a snack without taking a bath. This would only have strengthened David's belief that "I can do whatever I want to and no one can stop me." In other words, he would have his cake and eat it too. Mother played into the power struggle at first by trying to beat David in the chase, but she soon realized she could not overpower him and withdrew from the struggle. Mother's action of putting David to bed without his snack was appropriate in this situation and helped David to realize that he cannot always have things go his way simply because that's the way he wants them. David looked forward to snack time after his bath, but since he refused to cooperate and took up too much time in the "bathtub chase," there was no time for snacks.

To attain *power* is the second mistaken goal of children's misbehavior. If attention-getting behaviors do not succeed for children, then power is usually the next step in gaining importance. "Only when I'm in a powerful position do I feel important" is the mistaken belief held by power-oriented children. The power tactics of children are endless and sometimes devastating to the parents. If power-oriented children lose the battle, they believe they have lost their importance and value as a person.

At one time or another we have all probably experienced a power struggle with our children, marriage partner, boss, or maybe our own parents. Can you think of a time when your mother or father asked you to do something and you wanted to do it your way? Could this have been a power struggle?

Four-year-old Amy is legally blind in both eyes and requires thick corrective glasses. Amy is a cute child who easily wins love and affection from everyone she meets. She is also "daddy's little princess" and acts like a princess as long as she gets what she wants. When Amy's father refused to buy her a stuffed animal, she immediately turned on the tears, expecting her father to give in. When she realized the tears were not having an effect, she turned and looked at her father, yelling, "I don't love you anymore. I hate you."

At first, Amy tried using "water power," and then resorted to stronger measures: "blackmail." She tried to exchange her love for the stuffed animal she wanted. How could daddy's little princess say what she said? Amy's power and personal worth were at stake. She had to give it her best shot!

"Since you didn't give me what I wanted, I'll show you" was the intent of her blackmail.

Parents need to remove themselves from the power contest to help their children realize that they are only battling with themselves. If we try to use force or power with a power-oriented child, it will only reinforce the child's efforts to maintain a powerful position. Even if parents are able to overpower children in a particular situation, they have still lost and have in no way helped to redirect their children's motivation. Whenever parents get upset, angry, or rattled and "lose their cool," their children view this as success. "Look at what I have been able to do—look at how uptight I got mommy" is how children perceive their power. It is futile to use power against power.

Ricky, age ten, a mongoloid child, stands firmly and yells "No" louder every time his father tells him it's time to leave for school: a power contest. Susie, age fourteen, a brain-damaged child, refuses to get herself dressed and sits on her bed in a squatting position because she doesn't want to go out shopping with her mother. She silently but physically challenges her mother's authority. This is a power contest. Billy, age five, a trainable retarded child, picks at his food during dinner time. At first, mother and father try to coax Billy into eating. Eventually, his parents threaten him and send him to his room without dinner: a power contest.

Parents get very mad and upset when their children openly defy them. Andrew, who has muscular sclerosis, throws a temper tantrum in the store when his mother refuses to buy him the toys he wants. Andrew is using a form of blackmail. How can mother deprive her child of a simple toy? Eventually under the pressure of Andrew's temper tantrum and the pressure from the onlookers, she will either give in to the blackmail or hurriedly take Andrew out of the store before her shopping is completed. Andrew has won in either case.

"Water power" is another means by which children try to conquer their parents. Parents often give in when children cry, and lack the courage to stand firm in their convictions. Children are well aware of their parents' limits and do not hesitate to push them to their breaking point if they know they will eventually achieve victory. We need to go one step beyond the limits our children set for us or learn to sidestep power struggles if we are to put an end to family feuding.

Children strive to gain power so they can feel important and secure. They use many power tactics to undermine their parents' willpower. Children can "turn off" to parents and become "parent deaf," acting as if they never hear them. Children can use "blackmail" to let their parents know what they can expect if certain demands aren't met. "Water power" often works. Open defiance will, in most cases, anger parents.

This second mistaken goal of children's misbehavior can also be recognized by how the parents feel. Parents will become angry and upset when caught in a power struggle. An additional clue to recognizing power struggles is finding ourselves trying to use force and demanding that our children do what *we* say. Whenever we feel the need to resort to the use of our own power, we can be pretty sure that we've been "hooked" again.

A final observation that we can make about power and what distinguishes power plays from attention-getting behaviors is the child's response to our actions. Attention-getting behaviors will temporarily stop when we take action. However, power struggles do not stop but become more intensified if we try to stop the misbehavior. For the time being it is sufficient that we are able to recognize power tactics. In the following chapters specific methods will be discussed for handling power struggles.

Revenge

Mother refused to give Paul more candy. He cried to get mom to give in to his demand. He then yelled and screamed at the top of his lungs. Mom still refused and removed herself from the room. When she returned, she found the bowl of sugar all over the floor. Mom was angry and hurt because of what he did to her.

Paul exhibited a typical behavior of a revengeful child. A revengeful child believes, "Since things are not done the way I want them to be, I will get back at people for not allowing me to do what I want to do." Of the four goals of misbehavior, *revenge* tends to be one of the most difficult to handle. Revengeful children have given up any hope of being accepted by people. They feel hurt and therefore react to people in a violent and disruptive manner. For parents and teachers, revengeful children are the most difficult to deal with.

To understand a revengeful child, we must consider that she often feels hurt. This hurtful feeling is often a product of her feeling unable to be appreciated by people. She does not feel that she can find her place in life in a positive manner.

The exceptional child is often seen as the different one. To many, being different may mean not being as good as the other children. Handicapped children are often not allowed to participate because people do not understand these children and their capabilities. Because they often see that they are treated differently, the children themselves may become resentful and act in a revengeful manner.

The main method of redirecting a revengeful child is to attempt to communicate to him that you love him and really appreciate him. The problem with this method is that it is very difficult to communicate love while a child is trying to make you feel bad or hurt you. Encouraging a child who doesn't feel he has a place is a very frustrating task. You must constantly keep in mind that when you respond to these children with resentment and revenge of your own, his view that no one really does appreciate him will be reinforced.

David, a ten-year-old, is always getting himself into some sort of mischief. He has been sent home from school so many times for disrupting class that his parents have been warned that he may face suspension. At home David thinks nothing of stealing from his parents' dresser or of breaking his little sister's toys. David's parents have tried spanking him and sending him to his room, but the destructive behavior continues. David hit his sister with one of her toys, causing her to be taken to the hospital emergency room. His parents are extremely upset at what happened to their daughter, but they are more hurt by what David has done than anything else. They just can't understand what made David do such a terrible thing.

When we try to understand the purpose of such behavior, we can clearly see that David has succeeded in his retaliation against his parents. Nothing could have hurt his parents more.

What leads children to act in a revengeful manner? To feel so unloved? David was given everything he could want. His parents never denied him any of his requests, and he had free rein in the house. David's parents, out of guilt, tried to compensate for David's handicap by giving him everything. However, when David's little sister was born, things began to change. His parents could no longer give him their undivided attention or provide the service that he demanded. As David tried harder and harder to keep things as they were, to have everything revolve around him, he grew more discouraged and began to feel that he wasn't getting everything he deserved. He felt unloved and blamed his parents. David moved away from his struggle for power, since it didn't get him the payoff he thought it would, and tried getting back at his parents—revenge.

Once we are able to determine David's behavior as revengeful, we can see how he has developed some of his beliefs. We can now understand why spanking and threats have no useful effect. The more David was punished for his misbehavior, behavior he thought was his right—that he could do as he pleased—the more he began to feel unloved and unfairly treated. This feeling caused him to become even more destructive and brought more punishment. Eventually a cycle of behavior was formed. David, like all revengeful children, needs discipline, not punishment. He needs to feel loved and needs opportunities in which he can find his place in the family through constructive behavior.

When we become aware of revengeful behavior, we need to keep in mind the child's reasoning and the purpose of such action. If we can do this, we can learn to redirect revengeful behavior.

Revenge can take all forms. In David's situation it involved physical reaction. This physical reaction is also exhibited by Dale, who constantly attacks his brothers and sisters whenever they build a puzzle or paint a picture for mom and dad. Dale feels that he doesn't get the same reaction and resents his brothers and sisters because they are the "good" kids in the family.

Revenge can also take the form of very disruptive behavior. James resented being told to turn the lights off when he left the room or to turn off the television and radio when he was finished. He began to unplug the appliances in the house, including the clocks and lights. He also unplugged the refrigerator and the freezer and most of the food in the house spoiled. This type of revenge often results in the loss of property.

Psychological revenge is one of the most difficult types of revenge to understand. The result may be that the parent feels very bad. Although revenge is very close to power seeking in many ways, the purpose of the revengeful child is to get back at and *hurt* the parent.

In the previous two mistaken goals, attention and power seeking, we analyzed the feeling parents had toward those misbehaviors. The parents' emotional reaction toward attention-getting behaviors is frustration and annoyance. Parent's emotional reaction to power struggles is anger. When James tried to get back at his parents by pulling out all the electrical plugs, his parents experienced the emotional reaction of feeling hurt. These emotional reactions are one way of determining the child's mistaken goal.

Lee, a dyslexic child, resented any reprimand, especially when others could see or hear. One day when Lee came home late, mother told her that she couldn't go outside until she could get home on time. Lee responded to her confinement by telling her father how cruel mother is and that she treats Lee differently from the other children because she has problems. Lee attempted to achieve psychological revenge by punishing her mother for disciplining her. She achieved this by telling her father, "Mother doesn't love me."

The child attempts to get even with the parents by verbally attacking emotionally sensitive areas. "I don't love you anymore" may be a way of establishing power, but it is often used to hurt the parents and is therefore also a revengeful action.

Inadequacy

In chapter 4 we mentioned Ed, a child with a hearing problem. He was able to manage satisfactorily in school for five years without anyone realizing he had a difficulty. When Ed and his classmates entered their new open classroom, he began to fall behind in his schoolwork to such a great extent that he didn't want to go to school. He would cry every morning, whining that he hated school, and he even attempted to destroy his school books. Ed consistently encountered failures and saw no hope for success.

This situation illustrates the fourth mistaken goal of children's misbehavior —*inadequacy*. Encountering one failure after another, Ed began to feel inadequate and not OK about himself. He believes, "There is no hope, I'm totally useless, so why should I even try? I'm only going to meet with failure."

Many exceptional children who have this or a similar belief begin to exhibit behavior that makes those around them adopt a hopeless attitude. Children who believe they are inadequate at performing tasks have encountered discouraging situations that reinforce their view of themselves. Once this has occurred, children may either exaggerate a real disability or actually devise a debilitating behavior to avoid situations where failure can occur. The purpose of inadequacy is to avoid any responsibility for oneself and to avoid being placed in success-failure situations.

We often see children like Alex who exhibit various learning difficulties in school, especially in reading. Alex was three months premature at birth, and at nine years of age he is still extremely small. He was referred because of excessive fighting with the other children, tearing up books, and general disruptive behavior. At first glance Alex appears to have a lot of power and revenge. When we talked with Alex and observed him at home and school, it became evident that his aggressive behaviors mask a generalized feeling of inadequacy. Both his learning problems and his size contribute greatly to his feelings of being different. He's never big enough, strong enough, or smart enough compared with how he feels he's supposed to be. His high level of frustration is indicative of how much pressure he puts on himself to perform. Yet he is never able to perform up to his standards, and therefore he becomes more frustrated. When Alex is frustrated, he often sits out as a means to cover up his inadequacies. Since he cannot be the best at being good, he attempts to be the best at being bad—especially in school, where he has not been able to find his place through academic achievement.

Many exceptional children may see themselves as failures because they are not always able to meet standards they feel they should meet. They are very likely to become discouraged. The use of encouragement is the major way parents can combat the feeling of inadequacy in their children (see chapter 8).

Although we as parents may try to assist our children who appear to be inadequate or helpless at a task, eventually we may throw our hands up in despair. This, of course, is the danger for children who fall into inadequacy. We must all be aware of this, for when we throw our hands up in despair and begin to believe that the situation is hopeless, we reinforce this same belief in our children. It is difficult not to experience this hopelessness, the emotional response within us by which we can recognize our child's mistaken goal of inadequacy, since these children actually do strive to prove that they are helpless. From their viewpoint, it is less painful to give up than to meet with constant failure. Situations need to be found and sometimes purposely developed in which these children can experience some amount of success and not fear failure. We also need to realize that giving up on our children will not help them or lessen our frustrations. Even when we feel ourselves running out of gas, we need to go that extra mile to help disprove our children's mistaken beliefs. Because their purpose is to have us give up on them and reinforce their belief of "I'm not OK," we must maintain a conscious awareness of this fact.

To find the road to redirecting our children's misbehaviors, we need a map. We need to find a way to understand the various disruptive behaviors that our children may exhibit to discover the appropriate corrective measures. A library catalogues its books. Without this system it would be virtually impossible to find what we wanted. The behaviors children exhibit also need to be catalogued according to their purpose. For without any system of understanding children's behavior, parents would be dealing with their children by trial-and-error. It would be like going from shelf to shelf hoping to find the book you want. Knowing that all children's behavior has a purpose and can be catalogued according to the mistaken goal, we can avoid going in circles and we can increase our effectiveness as parents.

8

ENCOURAGEMENT: Building the Positives

One of the most important child-rearing principles discussed in this book is *encouragement*. So often we overlook giving recognition to our children for their positive behavior or for progress they have made. In trying to correct or diminish behavior we fall into the common trap of concentrating our efforts on countering negative behavior. Handling misbehavior effectively is a large part of raising children well, but we must also build on existing positive behavior. Encouragement reinforces our children in appropriate behavior. Encouragement is the key to building courage, to inspiring the feeling of being OK, and to strengthening our children's ability to deal with problems they encounter in life.

Right now you are probably telling yourself, "Oh, I praise my child when he does well," or, "I tell my daughter she's a good girl for eating all her food." You may indeed acknowledge accomplishments your children make. However, there are two crucial points which need to be emphasized:

First, how does your recognition of your child's good behavior compare with your recognition of his misbehavior? We may find ourselves making more of a fuss and commotion over the destruction than over the cooperative behavior.

Jeffrey has been learning to feed himself and is doing well at learning this new skill. While eating dinner Jeffrey spilled some food on his clothes, and mother immediately reacted, "Oh, Jeffrey, look at what you've done. You got food all over yourself!"

Although Jeffrey has been doing well mother's reaction was discouraging instead of encouraging. Jeffrey's handicap is emphasized by the discouraging statement and the rest of the family's ability to do things he cannot. Mother could simply have helped Jeffrey clean himself up and commented, "We all make mistakes." Jeffrey would gain a feeling that mistakes are just part of being human and that no one is perfect whether handicapped or not. Part of encouraging children is our ability to refrain from being discouraging.

By our tone of voice, facial expressions, body gestures, and comments we can easily discourage our children without knowing it. By diminishing our discouraging actions, we can begin to build a more positive and encouraging relationship.

The second point to be emphasized is that praise is different from encouragement. We often hear parents say, "You're such a good boy for eating dinner," or, "What a good girl you are for dressing yourself!" On the surface these praise statements appear to be fine because they are positive. But if we examine praise statements a bit further, we might realize that we may be accidentally communicating a different message. What happens if Ralph *doesn't* eat all his food or what happens if Linda *doesn't* dress herself correctly? They may begin to believe that they are not worthwhile. Praise does not separate the "doer" from his act. Therefore, what we actually say when we use praise is: "We believe you're a good person because you've done something good." Conversely, when children do not perform up to par, they come to believe that they are bad. The child who fails logically concludes, "I'm good when I do well, therefore, since I have done bad, I'm no good." By using this form of praise, parents may fail to communicate what they truly believe when something does not go right—"I didn't like what you did, but I still like you."

Encouragement does separate the "doer" from her act and helps to eliminate the erroneous connection that may be made when praise is used. "Johnny, it's nice to see you enjoying dinner and being able to feed yourself." This statement doesn't relate Johnny's "goodness" or "badness" to finishing his dinner but rather encourages his efforts.

We look at our children and see them get upset and cry when they make mistakes, or we see children who don't want to try because they may not do well. Why do you think this occur? The explanation is simple. By using praise-oriented statements when our children perform a positive act, we're actually teaching them to fear poor performance. Encouragement diminishes children's fears of failure and allows them to attempt tasks even if they may not do as well as they would like. The encouragement process allows children to try out their skills regardless of limitations because their OK-integrity is not threatened.

Valerie's mother observes her making her bed for the first time. Although the corners are uneven and not properly tucked in, mother states, "I appreciate your helping me out with your room. It's really neat to see how you've learned to make the bed."

This statement encourages Valerie to try. It does not associate being a "good" girl with making the bed. Valerie will be more likely to feel like trying again because she is appreciated for her *effort*. Mother is right to make the encouraging statement now rather than waiting until Valerie makes the bed perfectly. It is the movement toward learning a new skill with which Valerie's mother is concerned. If Valerie's mother waits until she successfully completes the task of making the bed perfectly, Valerie may become discouraged in learning the task.

In the previous example, Valerie was encouraged for her participation, regardless of her skill level. Valerie can also be encouraged in such a way as to help increase her skill. Valerie's mother can say, "I appreciate your helping me out with your room. Can I help you with this and show you how to fix the covers?" Encouraging statements can be made even in the face of poor performance. Valerie is more likely to learn and more likely to develop courage to try new tasks because she does not fear being criticized for not doing well. Rather, she is encouraged for her efforts. Encouragement can be given at every step of the learning process, from our children's first attempt through the final step of accomplishment.

Following are ten examples of encouraging statements for you to examine. Five encouraging statements are compared with five praise statements, and five additional encouraging statements are given that have no counterparts.

Encouragement	*Praise*
1. I really appreciated your help in the supermarket today.	What a good girl you are for helping me in the supermarket!
2. Thank you for cleaning the living room. It looks very nice.	What a good boy you are for cleaning the living room!

3. You all played so nicely together while I was busy in the kitchen.

I'm so proud of the way all of you played together.

4. You certainly worked hard on your science fair project.

I felt so proud seeing your project at the science fair.

5. Thank you for helping me with the dishes.

Aren't you wonderful to be Mommy's little helper!

6. Why don't you try again? I'm sure you can do it. (After a child attempted to pour a glass of milk that spilled.)

7. It seems you're having some difficulty with school. Maybe we could sit down and discuss it. (After a child brings home a failing report card.)

8. I know you're unhappy with the way your project turned out. Have you learned anything you might do differently for next time?

9. It seems as though you had an accident. Would you like me to help you clean it up? (After a child accidentally breaks a vase.)

10. Whenever I make mistakes, I try to learn from them. What do you think you could learn from this situation? (After a child makes a mistake.)*

Encouraging statements require parents to be honest. As we begin to separate the "doer" from his act, we remove our need to look for good performances only as a prerequisite for positively oriented statements. When we are able to accomplish this in focusing upon the whole of our children's

*Taken from Yura, Zuckerman, Zuckerman, and Costa, *A Parents' Guide to Children: The Challenge* (New York: Hawthorn Books, Inc., 1978).

actions, encouraging statements come easier because they are honest. Statements that are not truly felt are easily recognized by our children as false and are often discouraging.

Mother responded to David's first attempt at clay pottery by saying, "That's beautiful." David could see that his attempt was not beautiful and, discouraged, threw it on the ground.

Mother's honest feeling was not that it was beautiful but rather that she was glad to see David enjoying his work with clay. Saying what she honestly felt would have been a truly encouraging statement for David.

In recent years we have observed parents reinforcing children with candy and other treats for positive behavior. These are known as primary reinforcers. Primary reinforcers are like praise in that they do not separate children from their actions. Careful consideration must be made in the use of primary reinforcers with exceptional children. Children often increase positive behavior only because they receive a reward. Because the positive behavior is a result of an external stimulus, such as food or money, this increase usually lasts for a short time only. The use of primary reinforcers should be limited because it does not make children increase certain behaviors out of self-satisfaction. Primary reinforcers may initially be used with more severely retarded children because they supply something tangible, which usually results in an immediate response. But they should be replaced as quickly as possible with verbal encouraging statements. Children never have enough encouragement, but they can tire of these treats.

Encouraging statements can be emphasized by positive physical contact from parents, showing the children the association between encouraging statements and our loving physical contact.

The emphasis of this chapter has been on the concept of encouragement. As we have seen, encouragement provides positive recognition for our children. The main purpose of developing an encouraging atmosphere is to assist children in their preparation for dealing with life's tasks. If we as parents provide an encouraging atmosphere rather than a critical one, we can prepare our children for the many disappointments that we all face in life. This is accomplished by instilling in our children the courage and self-confidence to try and to keep on trying. Whether one is handicapped or not, he must face the reality that there are others around him who perform various tasks better than he does. Encouragement teaches our children to perform at their highest level and to maintain a personal feeling of self-worth regardless of the superior performance of others around them.

The encouragement process is based upon being the best that one can be, rather than being better than someone else. In this way, we can all concentrate upon our assets and more easily accept our limitations. Encouragement is the foundation stone of a positive relationship with our children and the *motivator* for any behavior change in our children.

9

LOGICAL CONSEQUENCES

Ron Anderson's nine-year-old daughter never listened to anything he told her to do. She talked back and refused to mind him. At a meeting for parents of exceptional children Ron voiced his frustration about kids today and how hard it is to get them to listen. He explained that when he was a child, he would never have dared refuse to do what his parents had told him. He "learned the hard way" in life, and he just couldn't understand the rebelliousness of kids today. At one point during the discussion one of the parents asked Ron what he meant by "learning the hard way." Ron explained that he learned from his mistakes and didn't make the same mistake twice.

The other parents said, "Maybe you learned from the consequences of your behavior and your daughter will learn the same way. When you just tell her how she's supposed to act, she doesn't learn that way. Where there's a reasonable consequence that follows the behavior, she'll learn."

Ron stood there for a moment and realized that he was trying to help his daughter by telling her how to act. He realized that she needed to *see* the effect of her behavior on her actions. He now discovered why threats and punishment had not worked in the past.

Ron discovered that the best way to change a child's behavior is to use consequences that appear logical to the child. There must be a direct relationship between the consequence and the child's action. For example, Bonnie was told to turn off the TV and come to dinner. She continued watching until the program was over. When she entered the kitchen, she discovered that everyone had almost finished eating and the food was cold. Bonnie realized that she either had to go hungry or eat the cold food. Bonnie will most likely be more manageable in the future because the negative consequence is logical.

We often yell at and spank our children to get them to listen. But not until they are given the responsibility for their own behavior will they be able to modify their misbehavior.

The "power of the social order" uses the logical flow of things instead of power or force. We as adults know what to expect if we are told that we will be docked an hour's pay if we are a few minutes late for work. When we see our paycheck at the end of the week come up short, the consequence of our behavior becomes quite clear. Having the boss yell at us and criticize us for being late might not change our behavior if there is no difference in our paycheck. When there is a logical consequence that follows our misbehavior, we are more conscious of what we've done. When there is no logical consequence, we don't learn the effect of our behavior.

Jessica had been taking adaptive physical education at school. She really enjoyed the use of the trampoline. One night she discovered her bed was very similar to the trampoline. At first her mother yelled at her to stop jumping on the bed but she continued bouncing. Jessica continued until mother got so frustrated that she spanked her daughter. The jumping stopped temporarily but started again a short time later. After about a week of this, Jessica's parents were really frustrated. A counselor recommended that they use a logical consequence to solve the problem. The next time Jessica started jumping up and down, they came into the room and told her gently but firmly to stop. As usual, she continued. So they lifted her off the bed and put her on the chair. They began to take the bed apart. They removed the metal head and foot boards and the frame. They put the mattress and box spring on the floor. Jessica had a rude awakening—*thud*—she didn't bounce. The parents left the bed on the floor for a week, and then, put it together again. When Jessica saw the bed, she began bouncing again. So they disassembled it again for two weeks, then put it back together. Jessica began to bounce but realized what would happen: She stopped the bouncing without a word from mom. The problem was solved, since there was a consequence Jessica did not want. She realized that her bouncing on the bed caused the consequence.

The first step in establishing a logical consequence is for the parent to inform the child of what will happen if the misbehavior continues. Jessica was told that if she continued to bounce on the bed, it would be disassembled. By informing the child of the possible consequence, we make it apparent that he has a choice in determining the outcome of the situation. In a logical consequence the child is given an opportunity to choose between behaving properly or misbehaving. The decision is his.

Parents should not try to set up a logical consequence while still visibly angered by the misbehavior of the child. A time should be chosen to inform the child when the parent can approch the child in a pleasant manner.

The parents' pleasant manner when informing a child of a consequence is a vital component in the process of using logical consequences instead of punishment. This pleasant yet firm manner helps the child realize he is not being personally attacked. This feeling must be communicated for the logical consequence to work.

Rick has tried to think of a logical consequence for the children's fighting in the backseat of the car. He decides that he will pull off the road and inform them that they will have to sit there and possibly miss lunch unless they decide to stop fighting and act in a reasonable manner. However, by the time Rick pulls over, he is so irritated that he forgets the basic principle of firmness and pleasantness. He yells at the children, telling them that they will have to sit there and be quiet or else they will get no lunch. Rick's original idea was good, but because of his anger and yelling he has turned a good logical consequence into punishment. This could open the door for a power struggle. The more unpleasant the manner of informing the children of the future consequence of their behavior, the more the children will feel the consequence as a personal attack.

A mother was recently observed yelling at her son in a supermarket. She screamed and said, "If you do that one more time, I'll pull every hair out of your head." The child knows this would not happen and therefore it has no effect. This was an unrealistic consequence, which could not be carried out by the parent. The consequence needs to be realistic, and the parent must make a commitment to follow through with the agreed action.

Keith made it clear that he didn't like what was being served for dinner. He was told very nicely, "We're very sorry that you don't like anything we're having. You have a choice of trying to eat it or leaving the table and waiting to eat breakfast." Upon hearing more complaints Keith's parents asked him to leave the room if he couldn't conduct himself in a proper manner. They acted in a very pleasant yet firm manner and were prepared to follow through with the consequence of having him leave the table. It would have been easy for his parents to make something different for him or to make him sit there until he finished the meal, neither of which would place the responsibility on Keith for his behavior.

The underlying principle that makes the logical consequence work is the parents' ability to connect their action to the child's behavior in a way in which the child can see a logical relationship between the two. Informing a child that she cannot watch her favorite television show because she ate a piece of candy when she wasn't supposed to is not a logical connection of parental action and the child's behavior. This cannot be considered a logical consequence because there is no logical relationship between eating candy and television. The logical consequence would be the removal of candy from the house. The parent could state, "Since you're unable to control yourself and eat candy when you're not supposed to, we will not keep candy in the house until you think you are able to control yourself." A logical consequence should relate to the specific misbehavior exhibited. The removal of television can be viewed as a parental punishment for the child's defiance— the parents arbitrarily chose to take television away. The relevance of this to the misbehavior of eating candy is minimal and the impact on the misbehavior is lost because the parents did not take the time to develop a consequence that is directly connected to it.

Bill, who was issued his first parking ticket, a nonmoving violation, was informed when he went to pay the fine that he would lose his license for sixty days. It would be understandable to get angry in a situation like this. The consequence of having his license suspended was not justified because the consequence was not related to the action. It is easier for us to accept consequences which relate to our actions.

It is your responsibility to redirect your child's misbehavior by thinking of the best ways of obtaining long-lasting results. This is done by your developing consequences that logically follow the child's actions. You can develop a logical consequence if you keep in mind these basic principles: first, that the consequence is related to your child's action; second, that the consequence is established in a firm yet pleasant manner; third, that you are prepared to carry through with the consequence; last, that you try to inform your child of the consequence before taking action upon the misbehavior. These principles will allow your child to maintain his dignity. He will be able to assume the responsibility for his own actions. As a result there can be a positive and friendly relationship between you and your child.

Although it may be beneficial to follow the basic principles outlined here, one of these principles is not always practicial to use: Informing the child of the consequence before we act may not always be possible.

Martha is a nine-year-old child who has been accustomed to a lot of attention from her mother. One day, while her mother was finishing the dishes, Martha asked if they could play when she finished. Her mother explained that they had played earlier but she would play with her after she finished looking at the paper. Martha demanded that she play with her immediately. Mother did not respond to her daughter's yelling—she had already explained the situation. When she finished the dishes and went to the living room, the paper was gone. When she asked where the paper was, Martha said she took it because she wanted mother to play with her. After pursuing Martha to give her the paper, she began to do something else—mother couldn't think of a logical consequence, but she needed to communicate to Martha that her behavior was unacceptable.

The next day Martha came home for lunch, since she lived within walking distance of her school. When she entered the kitchen, Martha was surprised to find that there was no lunch on the table. Martha's mother explained the reason there was no lunch: She could not do her food shopping because the food coupons she normally used were in the paper. Since these coupons were very important to their budget, Martha's mother could not go to the store until she found the paper. Mother said, "We'll just have to eat some of these leftovers until I have a chance to get a paper and go to the store." Martha was upset because she realized how her misbehavior had affected her.

Martha's mother handled the situation well. She stopped when she did not know how to handle the situation. When she did find a way to react, there was a logical relationship between the consequence and the behavior; she dealt with the situation in a firm yet pleasant manner.

This situation did not allow the consequence to be prearranged as Martha's mother would have liked. Mother could not have known what was going to happen and therefore she couldn't have prepared for it. This type of situation is not common but should be kept in mind when using logical consequences. It is always best to inform the child of the consequences of misbehavior. We as parents must be aware of special circumstances that affect the implementation of these principles. It is important to understand that circumstances that may adversely affect other methods of discipline, such as physical disability, visual defects, or lower intellectual ability, do not necessarily detract from the use of logical consequence.

The communication of what is expected of the child may be done as it was with Jessica, a severely retarded girl, who was made to understand that bouncing on the bed was unacceptable. The parents used verbal comments to communicate what was expected. Even the simple use of no and then an action may be enough to show the connection between the behavior and the consequence.

A mother reported that her preschool daughter Sandy consistently left her toys all around the house. Mother had used various methods to solve the problem. She was constantly reminding her daughter to put her toys away. This was a daily routine. It got to the point where Sandy's mother resorted to spanking her and threatening her by taking television away if she didn't pick up her toys.

Mother's reaction is a common one. Although there were many punishments and threats, they had only a short-term effect on Sandy's behavior. This had been going on for a long time without any major change. Punishment doesn't work today with children—we all seem to use it at times, but the results are obvious: There is little long-term change in the behavior of the child, and we as parents become more and more tired from the battle.

We have emphasized in chapter 1 that our society is moving further away from autocratic structure to a more democratic social system. Punishment can be effective only in a society in which power is the accepted means of authority. In this type of authoritative social structure where power belongs to a few, the adults command authority over children, who have very little sense of equality. Relationships are based on the parents' being the ultimate authority in all situations. Parental authority is supported by a similar social atmosphere.

Today our society is oriented toward a belief in human rights and equality, creating a more overt democratic atmosphere. This atmosphere is predicated upon the concepts of mutual respect and dignity of the individual. Children have been recognized as having a place in this democratic system that is considered to be equal to that of adults. Parents are no longer superior to their children. Greater knowledge, physical strength, and size do not make one superior to another in regard to human rights. But although children have gained equal status with adults, they still require guidance and experience to learn.

A democratic society no longer supports the use of punishment, because that relies upon the belief that one person is superior to another. There is no place in a democratic society for the exercise of such power. Children instinctively realize how futile are parents' efforts to control them by the use of force, power, or fear. Children realize that a parent's reliance on power is no longer effective and they will no longer submit to these methods. Punishment only seems to teach them to use power to gain control over others. Then the war between parents and children escalates as children in turn become skillful at using the power that we have unintentionally taught them they have.   .

We need to replace punishment and other authoritarian methods with those based on more democratic ideals, such as mutual respect and cooperation. Logical consequences fit these conditions, allowing us to discipline our children in a manner based on cooperation and respect, invoking the authority of the social order rather than our individual authority or power.

Logical consequences can easily be distinguished from punishment:

Logical Consequences	*Punishment*
1. Arise from the power of the social order.	Arises from the individual authority or power.
2. May be prearranged between the parent and child.	Is not prearranged, carried out solely at the discretion of the parent.
3. Are carried out in a calm yet pleasant manner.	Is usually carried out in an angry, forceful manner.
4. Imply that the children make the choices.	Implies that parents make the choices for the children.
5. Teach children through experience.	Teaches children to use power to control others.
6. Teach self-respect and respect for others.	Disregards both self-respect and respect for others.

The situation we described with Sandy and her toys could have been handled differently by taking into consideration the various elements of a logical consequence. During a time of low frustration the mother could have discussed with Sandy the problem of picking up her toys. The mother's intentions could have been stated in a pleasant yet firm manner. Sandy could have been told that when she finished playing, she would have to put her toys away in their proper place. Sandy's mother might have said, "If you choose not to take care of them, I will have to put the toys away for one week. At the end of the week, you may have the toys back. It will be up to you how long this will continue."

The conditions that make this a logical consequence were:

1. There is a logical flow between Sandy's behavior and the consequence.
2. The mother explains the consequence to Sandy before taking the action.
3. The consequence is handled in a firm yet pleasant manner.
4. Sandy is given the opportunity to choose her course of action. (She may lose the use of the toys she doesn't put away or she can learn to put them away and thus retain total access to them.)
5. Sandy's mother shows respect for her daughter by treating her in a manner that allows her the freedom to choose to behave or not to behave.

Sandy's mother could show mutual respect by remaining calm and pleasant, not allowing herself to get upset. The control of behavior in a democratic society is best accomplished by allowing the power of the social order to take effect rather than utilizing personal power.

LIMITS TO LOGICAL CONSEQUENCES

These illustrations are not intended to picture logical consequences as a panacea for solving all misbehavior in our children. Although logical consequences are an extremely effective method for dealing with misbehavior in children, there are numerous occasions where the use of natural consequences (see chapter 10) may be the best approach. With the mistaken goal of attention getting, logical consequences tend to be the most effective. But caution needs to be used when devising logical consequences with power-oriented children, who are pursuing mistaken goal number two. This difficulty lies not with the technique, but rather with implementing logical consequences when one is angry. Since power-oriented children trigger feelings of anger, it is difficult for parents to remain pleasant, which is a necessary condition if a logical consequence is to work. When implemented by parents who are angry, logical consequences tend to be perceived by children as punishment.

It is also true that in many power situations parents run the risk of having a logical consequence backfire on them.

Mrs. Lindsay attempted to pick up her daughter, Ashley, from school. Ashley refused to go, saying, "I want to stay here and play with my friends." Mrs. Lindsay, having been in a parent group for exceptional children, tried to think of a logical consequence to use in this power situation. She gave her daughter the choice of either coming home with her or staying there. Ashley promptly turned and went back to play, infuriating her mother.

Mrs. Lindsay made one fundamental error. She gave two choices, neither of which was a negative consequence to Ashley. Allowing Ashley to stay at the school playground fulfilled her power demands. Power-oriented children will likely choose the opposite of what we want them to do because they believe that they only count when they're doing things *their way*. The choice is not whether to stay or go, but rather the choice of *how* you are to go! When Mrs. Lindsay first approached her daughter about leaving and she refused, she could have simply stated, "I know that you would like to stay and play with your friends, but I'm afraid we must leave. Since we must go, you can either walk to the car or you'll have to be taken to the car. The choice is yours."

Power-oriented children present so many unique situations that we have to keep in mind a few basic points when you find yourself in a power struggle.

1. Don't give choices that can't be carried out.
2. Don't give a choice if you can't accept the consequence.
3. Don't give choices that you feel may be physically harmful.
4. Don't give choices when you are angry.

Billie was in the special class for retarded children who were receiving swimming lessons at the local pool. After the lesson the lifeguard asked the children to leave the pool. Billie refused to leave and said, "You can't make me."

Because of the danger to himself and the other children, the lifeguard told Billie to leave or be removed; Billie forced him to go into the pool and remove him.

After he was removed, Billie was told that the following week he would not be allowed in the pool. This was the rule for anyone who didn't leave the pool when the whistle was blown. Although he was angered by the situation, he understood that his remaining out of the pool was a consequence of his violating an important safety rule.

This situation utilized all the basic cautions. A choice was given, the choice could be carried out, physical danger was taken into consideration, and the action was carried out in a gentle yet firm manner.

When you find yourself in a power struggle with a child, the use of logical consequences may not be the best choice of action. The power-oriented child may interpret the consequence as punishment and feel as though her freedom of choice has been denied. The anger provoked in parents by these children is a further reason to be cautious when you attempt to impose a logical consequence in a power situation. These considerations are mentioned not to scare you away from using logical consequences but rather to assist you in their most effective use.

Precautions should be taken in the use of logical consequences with children who exhibit revengeful behavior, mistaken goal three. Children carry out acts of revenge because they believe others have treated them unfairly. It is because of this belief that revengeful children can misinterpret logical consequences as unfair acts of retaliation. They view the logical outcomes of their actions as parental retaliation. This perception is of course inaccurate, but ironically, it logically fits and supports their illogical beliefs.

It will take some time to feel comfortable and confident in setting up logical consequences. You will be unable to carry out logical consequences with 100-percent effectiveness. Nor should you expect such perfection. As you learn new principles in training your children, you find yourselves going through a training period. As with all new skills, you improve from practice, patience, and the courage to learn from your mistakes as you go through this retraining process.

In attempting to implement logical consequences for children with mistaken goals, certain conditions should be maintained to make this technique as effective as possible. Make sure that the consequence *is* logical; initiate the consequence in a gentle, not angry, manner; and communicate to the child the possible consequence before you take the action. In a democratic society logical consequences assist parents in redirecting misbehavior in their children while still maintaining a positive relationship between their children and themselves.

10

NATURAL CONSEQUENCES

Sharon, age ten, had a bad habit. She refused to keep her shoes on when she was outside. Sharon came into the house one day before supper crying about the dog. Mother's first thought was that a dog had chased or had bitten her, but she finally learned that the dog had chewed up her daughter's favorite sneakers, which were on the pavement. Mother asked Sharon, "How did the dog get them?" Sharon stated that she had left them outside and forgot to bring them in the house. Mother replied, "I'm really sorry that happened. What do you think we could do so this doesn't happen again?"

At first glance we may feel sorry for Sharon because her favorite sneakers were ruined. Yet, upon closer examination of this situation, we should not punish the dog or feel sorry for Sharon: There is no need, for this was a natural consequence of Sharon's behavior. She was told not to leave her belongings outside because they may become damaged in some way, but the effect of mother's warning had little impact on Sharon. The consequence occurred without mother's intervention, having a greater impact on Sharon because it occurred naturally.

Natural consequences demonstrate reality and its effects. When natural consequences occur, parental intervention is not necessary.

Freddie was late and missed his ride to the Little League game. The consequence of not being able to play occurred without any adult intervention. Natural consequences of this nature are effective because the responsibility for the consequence rests solely on the child, and is a natural result of the child's behavior.

Freddie's lesson would be diminished if his parents, upon learning what happened, had said "I told you so," given him a lecture, or punished him for missing his ride. Sharon's mother enhanced the lesson Sharon learned by asking her what she could do next time to avoid this happening again. This type of response allows the child to suffer the natural consequence without the parent-child relationship being adversely affected. The consequences which had befallen Freddie did not need to be reinforced by a lecture; in fact, a lecture would have diminished the effectiveness of the consequence by having the parents get involved unnecessarily. Freddie would perceive a lecture as "rubbing it in," which may develop needless resentment.

Logical consequences can always backfire. With natural consequences, however, since the parent does not get involved, there is minimal chance of it backfiring on the parent.

Some natural consequences are potentially dangerous or harmful, resulting in bodily injury, and should always be avoided.

Randy can get out of the fenced-in backyard and run into the busy street, where getting hurt is a natural consequence. Since we must not let Randy be injured in the street, we need to take another course of action, yet one that would develop a logical consequence of Randy's action. His father might tell Randy, "Since you're not able to remain in the yard and play, you will have to come in the house until you think you can play outside without leaving the yard."

Natural consequences may sometimes lead to physical discomfort for the child.

Roy was continually fighting, and one day he received a black eye and bloody nose. The parents could not have become involved even if they had wanted to, since this took place on Roy's way home from school. The natural consequence of fighting may be considered positive in Roy's case because it occurred naturally, without any parental intervention, and there was no real physical harm to the child.

For Roy this natural consequence was sufficient to deter future fighting.

There are many children who may continue to fight while encountering the same natural consequence. For some children the consequence may be a means of fulfilling their mistaken goal rather than modifying it.

It may be necessary for us to allow a certain amount of physical discomfort or unpleasant consequences to occur to our children. This is sometimes the only method for teaching them what their behavior means. We may rob our children of a valuable learning experience by not allowing them to experience the natural results of their actions, whether physically discomforting or not. Many parents protect their exceptional children from any discomfort, since they already have to cope with their handicaps. As parents, we do have a responsibility to inform our children of the possible natural consequences to their actions. Since we cannot be with our children all the time, it is impossible to protect them from unpleasant outcomes even if we wanted to. But it is not our responsibility to protect our children from the realities of life. We need to lend our guidance in a manner that will enable our children to learn to deal with life's tasks. Denying our children the reality of natural consequences is denying them a part of life. The more we try to protect our children from negative outcomes, the more difficult it will be for them to deal adequately with future discomforting and frustrating situations.

One may begin to question if there is a distinction between natural consequences and punishment. The distinction definitely exists. Natural consequences do not necessarily result in negative outcomes, whereas punishment is always negative. More important, however, is the fact that punishment is a retaliatory action taken by the parents. It is an exhibition of parental power and authority, and it always requires the involvement of an individual who assumes the role of a superior and more powerful being. Natural consequences, however, in no way express parental power, but only the power of reality. They allow children to learn the needs of the situation without parental involvement or action.

A child is told once by his mother not to touch the iron while she is using it. But he can't resist this new object and burns his finger. He has experienced the natural consequence of his behavior, as does the child who chooses to leave her bicycle outside even though mother has stated that it can get damaged. The child eventually discovers her bicycle has become rusted from the weather. A natural consequence is also experienced by the child who is outside for a short period of time dressed improperly. She comes in to change clothes because she is uncomfortable. A child who keeps his bedroom in disarray experiences a natural consequence when he can't locate his other sneaker. Electing not to eat dinner but to stay outside and play with friends. the child soon experiences hunger. The natural consequence, missing one meal and waiting until the next, results in hunger.

Vicky, age seven, has for the longest time refused to clean up her room. Mother and father have agreed to stay out of the situation to allow Vicky to feel the natural consequence of keeping a messy room. One night after the family had gone to the movies Vicky fell asleep. When the family arrived home, mother carried Vicky into the house. While carrying Vicky into her bedroom, mother tripped over something left on the floor, falling onto the bed. Vicky was awakened with a start. Mother explained that she had tripped over something on the floor.

Vicky's mother and father later reported that this natural consequence did have an effect on Vicky. Although her room still wasn't as neat as they wanted, Vicky did remove her belongings that were lying on the floor. Her room was much neater than before. Vicky's parents were able to understand that an orderly bedroom was a personal need of theirs but that this need not be expressed to teach Vicky the meaning of order. It appears that Vicky learned from the natural consequence and began to deal with the situation accordingly.

Rebecca, age eleven, has an orthopedic handicap and refuses to use her crutches. She prefers to be carried. Mother has been informed that Rebecca is capable of managing on her own but is choosing not to whenever someone is around to carry her. One morning when mother was going to drive Rebecca to school, Rebecca stood on the porch waiting for mother to carry her to the car. Mother told Rebecca that she would have to walk to the car if she wanted to go to school, and then she waited in the car for Rebecca. After Rebecca stood for some time, hoping mother would carry her, her legs and muscles began to ache. Rebecca eventually walked to the car because of the pain from standing too long.

Mother had to remain out of the situation to allow the natural consequence to take effect. It is difficult at times for parents to do as Rebecca's mother did. Staying out of a situation and knowing that a certain amount of physical discomfort will occur to the child is difficult. However, when Rebecca experienced the natural consequence of her action, she began to change her behavior to avoid any continued discomfort.

Natural consequences are probably the most useful teaching technique available to parents. We should not feel guilty because we allow our children to experience natural consequences—we are simply allowing our children to learn from reality. When we use natural consequences, we should also use our parental discretion to prevent any real physical danger. It is only natural for parents to want to protect their children. But our children can learn as we did, from mistakes. Learning the hard way teaches our children the basic rules of nature.

Factors to Be Maintained in Raising Exceptional Children

11

AVOID DRASTIC
ROUTINE CHANGES

Mrs. Roberts and Mrs. Barill are the teachers of an intermediate special education class. As one of their classroom activities they organized a field trip, a ferryboat ride. The trip had been planned for weeks and the children were excited. During the course of the ride Melvin wanted to climb the steps to see where the captain steered the boat. Melvin was afraid of very loud sounds, and as the teacher assisted him up the steps, the captain blew the whistle. Melvin became so frightened that he let go of the handrail and fell backward onto the teacher. He was so startled by the whistle that he also soiled his pants.

Any child put in a situation like Melvin's, who doesn't know what to expect, could easily be frightened. Children need to know what to expect if they are to feel secure. This sense of security is necessary for proper adjustment in life. Not knowing what to expect, Melvin lost his sense of security, which is maintained by certain known boundaries and expectations.

Developmentally disabled children rely heavily upon a sense of routine and order. The more inconsistent and irregular the daily pattern, the greater the difficulty for these children to know what is expected. Without a routine they are easily confused, get overexcited, and are often highly emotional, which makes it difficult to deal with them. It is important for us as parents to recognize the effect that routine has upon our children.

The situation that caused Melvin such difficulty could easily have been avoided with some simple preparation. Knowing that Melvin and the other children needed to know what to expect, the teacher could have prepared for the field trip. Those things that would have been different and nonroutine for them should have been discussed before the trip. The children could have been told that when they saw another boat, the captain would blow his whistle. They might have explained that this is how two boats say hello to each other. This simple explanation may have alleviated the surprise of the unexpected and loss of security experienced by Melvin and the other children.

We can understand why children get upset and confused at a change in their basic schedule and routine. Most of us have experienced this ourselves—on vacation, we can remember difficulty in sleeping or digestion because of the changes in our routine. We often see advertisements suggesting that we take Pepto Bismol along on the trip. These physical changes are our body's reaction to the changes in schedule. For we rely upon a schedule, and no matter how irregular it seems, it is a set routine. Even though we as adults may expect changes in our schedule, we still experience difficulty; children often do not know what to expect.

One of the most important factors in raising our children is the maintenance of a consistent daily routine from breakfast to bedtime. The importance of schedules for children can be observed in young children: As feeding time approaches, we can observe them sucking in preparation for being fed, even when they're sleeping. This routine behavior occurs because children develop a sense of security around their daily schedule, and that routine needs to be maintained as our children grow.

Maintaining a routine is usually complicated by summer vacation. The potential for confusion in some children may be greater during summer. It is during this time that all semblance of a routine tends to disappear. Bedtime, rising time, mealtime, chore time, homework time, all become irregular. As a result the feeling of security and order breaks down, and children may regress in previously gained skills. Leon (page 23) made progress in the use of eating utensils and general self-help skills during the school year. But his schedule changed drastically during summer vacation, and the consistent routine of practicing his self-help skills at mealtime was not maintained by his parents. Thus, Leon returned to school with the same low level of self-help skills he had before the instructions began. The skills that he learned were maintained by the routine of consistent practice. Thus, the irregularity in his summer schedule caused confusion, resulting in the loss of his newly acquired skills.

Even in the summer a routine must be maintained. Parents often mistakenly perceive summertime as a play time or a time for children to be free from all school and domestic obligations. They somehow believe that the joys of summertime will be diminished if a routine is maintained.

The routines, however, should not be complicated. The less complex the routine, the more able the child will be to know what to expect and, therefore, to begin to develop a positive sense of order within himself. An effort should always be made to inform the child of unexpected temporary changes in routine or plans. This explanation should be made in a simple and factual manner, and we should remember that children take their cues from their parents' reactions. The more upset, disturbed, or irritated the parents become at a change in routine, the more likely children will be upset. We should try to maintain a calm and positive attitude during unexpected routine changes. Although we all experience and appear to adjust easily to changes in our daily routine, adjustment does not come easily to exceptional children. It is for this reason that parents need to realize the priority of maintaining as consistent a routine as possible.

12

CONSISTENCY:
The Key Factor in Changing Misbehavior

In a parent study group for parents of exceptional children, a father was discussing his eight-year-old multiply handicapped boy named Tom, who had taken up disturbing behavior: Tom had recently begun hitting his head and fists on the walls. The parents' initial reaction was to yell at him to stop. He still hit himself five or six times a day; their reaction grew more intense. They vacillated between spanking Tom for his head banging and restraining him. By the third day Tom was hitting his head about fifteen to twenty times a day, and the parents put a helmet on his head to protect him from any physical damage.

The group attempted to discover the purpose for this behavior and discussed what might make the behavior worse. They decided that Tom had discovered through trial and error how his parents reacted to the head banging, and his behavior became a good attention-getting device. As Tom's behavior increased, the parents' involvement increased. Tom discovered that as he wanted more of his parents' attention, he need only bang his head more. The parents understood how this attention-getting behavior began, but it was difficult to deal with because of the potential physical harm to Tom.

A systematic corrective procedure was devised so that the parents would not provide the undue attention that Tom sought. The parents were informed of what would be likely to occur when they began ignoring the previously reinforced attention-getting behavior. The head banging would initially increase because Tom would expect their involvement, and would try harder to get his parents to respond in their usual manner. He would maintain his increased misbehavior until he realized that the payoff—attention—was no longer given for the misbehavior.

Although an increase in the incidence of misbehavior often is the immediate result of an implemented corrective procedure, the increase will diminish once the child realizes the parents are remaining firm and consistent in ignoring the misbehavior. When Tom's parents first tried the recommendation discussed in the parent study group, his head banging showed a drastic increase during the first two days to about thirty bangs a day, and then to about fifty per day. Although Tom's parents were told what to expect and to prepare themselves, it was extremely difficult to maintain consistently what they consciously knew was correct. There was a drastic change on the fourth day: Tom banged his head only three or four times, and this was the level of incidence throughout the remainder of the week.

In the next parent study group meeting, Tom's parents said, "We thought it was crazy, but the recommendation worked perfectly. The idea that the misbehavior would increase seemed more than we could handle until we realized that Tom wanted the attention no matter how negative. He was testing our consistency by increasing the behavior. We knew if we remained consistent in our ignoring and did not reinforce the attention getting, that the head banging would eventually diminish."

If parents understand the idea that things will get worse before they get better, it can actually be encouraging to them. It lets them know that their consistency is a redirective procedure. The child increases his misbehavior to wear the parents down and return the situation to the way it used to be. If the parents can maintain their redirective behavior, there is a good probability that the child's misbehavior will soon diminish. Parents increase their probability of diminishing their child's negative behavior through *consistency* rather than through trial and error. The consistency establishes the sense of order needed by all children and lets them know what is expected of them and what to expect from their parents.

Brenda has repeatedly been told to come to dinner when called. She is usually playing outside when her mother calls her. Mother repeatedly says that if she doesn't come in now, they'll put the food on the table and she'll have to eat cold food. Brenda rarely responds to her mother's calls and eats whenever she feels like it. The mother has never followed through with allowing Brenda to eat cold food, so it is understandable that Brenda doesn't change her behavior. Brenda is aware that she can disregard what her mother says because her mother has failed to follow through.

When there is no consistent parental action, the child feels no sense of respect for the boundaries that have been established. Inconsistencies ultimately bewilder and confuse the child. The child's sense of order and need for security warrants consistent parental action.

Although Brenda's mother was consistent in not following through with what she stated, there was an inconsistency between her actions and her verbal statements. This consistent training in the belief that yes means no and no means yes will inevitably confuse Brenda when she deals with reality outside the home.

We have all heard comments similar to that of the parent who said to her child at the supermarket, "If you touch one more thing I'll pull every hair out of your head." Obviously the parent was not going to do what she said. A prime rule when redirecting children's misbehavior is only to state those things that can realistically be carried out.

The Lynch family rarely enjoyed family outings such as picnics because the children constantly fought in the car. The parents threatened for years to do something about it, but they never followed through with any of their statements. Through parent study groups they realized that their threats were meaningless and unrealistic. One day on the way to a picnic at a local park the children began their fighting in the car. The parents immediately pulled over to the side of the road and informed the children that if the fighting continued, they would have to go back home because it was distracting and dangerous to everybody in the car. The children temporarily stopped the misbehavior, but after a few minutes they began again. Without comment, the parents turned around and proceeded home. When the children realized what was happening, they questioned the parents' action. The parents stated that they were sorry that the children did not want to go on a picnic but hoped that the next time they would behave in a more reasonable manner.

The parents showed respect for themselves by following through with their stated action. Their consistency allowed the children to learn what was expected from them and how they could find their place in the family in a positive manner. The inconsistent action of Brenda's parents virtually allowed her to do anything she wanted. In the Lynch family the children knew where they stood because the parents followed through with what they had said.

When we are trying to redirect children's behavior, we need to realize that the misbehavior developed over time, so we also need to allow a reasonable length of time for new methods to become effective. If the parents are consistent over a period of time, they allow children to adjust to new boundaries and develop a sense of order.

Ruth spent the majority of her time stopping fights between her two children, and periodically she would become exasperated. Ruth finally realized that their fighting was an attention-getting device that usually increased when she got involved. She decided to remove herself as much as possible or have the children leave the room until they were able to work out their differences. After a few weeks of Ruth's uninvolvement, there was a drastic decrease in the length and intensity of the quarrels. One day, while Ruth was talking with a neighbor, the children began fighting. Ruth was embarrassed at their behavior, and without thinking she yelled at the children.

Ruth's logic had been correct. She understood the purpose of the fighting, and withdrew the attention the children sought. But when she became involved just once, the children learned how far they would have to go to get their mother's attention. Ruth may consistently handle the situation correctly a hundred times, but if on the hundred first she falls apart and reverts to old unproductive ways, she must begin again. Children discover their parents' limits and push to reach them. Parents must recognize their limits and work at extending them. The sooner children realize that parents mean what they say and that they are consistent in their actions, the more readily the misbehavior tends to diminish.

In the previous example, Ruth did a fine job dealing with her children's fighting until she became concerned with what her neighbor would think if she ignored the situation. Our concern about what grandparents, neighbors, friends, and others think of our child-rearing practices should be monitored carefully. We may find that our children capitalize on our sensitivities in this area. Children have the uncanny knack of picking inappropriate times to misbehave—they quickly learn when we are most vulnerable, and most parents are vulnerable in the presence of others. But corrective measures must be consistent, even then, when it may be most difficult.

Some misbehavior affects others around us. There is a simple solution that will lessen the inconvenience. Linda, who lived in an apartment house with thin walls, was embarrassed at her child's violent temper tantrums. She decided to inform her neighbors of her attempts to stop the misbehavior by lessening her attention and involvement. They understood and she was less embarrassed. Since consistency is the key, the temporary inconvenience experienced by others should not outweigh the importance of parental consistencies in redirecting children's misbehavior.

13

A STITCH IN TIME SAVES NINE

We have all heard the expression, "A stitch in time saves nine," yet we rarely think of this expression as important in raising children. However, as a problem arises, if we act while the problem is small, we can avoid putting excess time and energy into solving a greater problem in the future. Preventive maintenance, whether it be of our homes, cars, or even our bodies, can save inconveniences in the future. Resting, drinking fluids, and taking aspirin at the first sign of a cold often help to prevent a more serious illness. Parents can utilize this same principle in child rearing.

Parents of older children indicate that their children experienced the "terrible twos," "rotten threes," and "horrendous fours." These same children at age fourteen and fifteen often use the same types of misbehaviors that met their needs in earlier years. Parents may believe that those past misbehaviors were indicative of normal stages of development. Actually, at an early age children are testing out behaviors, and they will continue these throughout their life if they help attain the goal they seek. Many misbehaviors that parents deal with as the child gets older could have been avoided or modified if they had been dealt with when they were initially observed. With aid from the hindsight of others we can learn to redirect children's misbehavior at its early stages rather than expending greater energy with less result at a later time.

Jonathan was a six-year-old boy who had difficulty controlling his bowel movements. The parents assumed that because their child was physically impaired, he was unable to control himself. Their physician stated repeatedly that she did not believe the problem was related to the physical impairment. The parents assumed that, although it was a problem and a source of irritation to the school, it would eventually work itself out. They continued to clean him up and didn't try to develop a systematic corrective action.

It is reasonable for parents of exceptional children to question the relationship between their child's misbehavior and his handicap (see chapter 3). However, when they learn that the misbehavior is not related to any lag in the developmental stage, nor is it caused by the child's handicap, it is necessary for them to initiate corrective action.

Because of various feelings such as guilt and overprotection (see chapter 5), many parents postpone corrective actions, which only enhances the difficulty of redirecting the misbehavior. Parents of exceptional children need to guard themselves against letting their emotions and feelings of guilt control their actions. Putting off necessary corrective measures communicates to these children that because of their handicap they have license to misbehave. The behavior typically is not tolerated when exhibited by the other children, but it is tolerated in exceptional children because of their handicap. By taking the necessary action to correct our children's misbehavior when it occurs, we give our children a sense of order and the feeling of being equally respected family members. When the exceptional child is treated like everyone else, it increases the probability that she will have a healthier self-image and a healthier outlook toward others.

14

ACTIONS SPEAK LOUDER
THAN WORDS

Charlie is a factory worker who asked his boss for a raise. His boss agreed that he was eligible and deserved a raise. Charlie was excited about the possibility of receiving a larger paycheck, and he eagerly awaited the increase. When he opened his pay envelope, he was shocked to discover that no raise was included. When he questioned his boss concerning the money, his boss indicated that it would be taken care of by next week. But next week came and the salary was still the same. Charlie no longer responded with enthusiasm.

Probably most of us have experienced ordering some product from a local store and being told that we'd get it the next day. After several phone calls and numerous promises we realize the order was not sent as promised. We come to doubt the veracity of what we are told from that point on.

Doubting the validity of what you've been told is understandable. There is an obvious discrepancy between what is *said* and what is *done*.

After being told the same thing over and over without seeing any results, we begin to disbelieve what is being said and respond purely to the actions taken. If Charlie had seen his raise or if we had received our product on time, we would know that they meant what they said because they followed through with their promise. The only time words have meaning is when they are supported by action. The more we *follow through* with what we say, the more likely people will know we mean what we say.

This same principle holds between parents and children. As parents attempt to correct children's misbehavior and enhance their positive behavior, consistent actions become necessary to make the words meaningful. Words have no meaning to children unless they are able to associate something with them: The word *toy* has no meaning unless we know that a toy is something with which we play. The word *no* means nothing unless the action is stopped. It is imperative that when we say something to children, we incorporate an action. In this way children learn the meaning of what we say and what is expected. The children gain a sense of security and order when they experience the congruency between the parents' words and their actions.

Parental action is of paramount importance with exceptional children. Exceptional children do need special assistance from their parents. However, this often communicates the idea that others will always be around to do things for them, which can hinder the development of independence. Parents sometimes overassist their children, even when children no longer need assistance. These parents want their children to develop new independent skills, but they continue to alleviate their children's frustration. Parents who wish to foster independence in their children must follow through with actions. And parental actions are especially important to exceptional children because they are generally used to and expect special assistance. The transition from dependence to independence must be supported by consistent parental action in order to be meaningful to exceptional children.

Tammy had difficulty learning how to control her hands when she dressed herself. It was not uncommon for her to have her coat on backward or incorrectly buttoned, but with time and special assistance she began to show mastery of these basic self-care skills. Although she was able to perform tasks regularly, Tammy would often come to mother saying she couldn't do it and that she needed help. She wanted her to do it for her. Mother would tell her that she was capable of doing it herself and that she should try. However, mother would eventually help her put on her clothes.

Mother's encouraging words about her daughter's ability to put on her clothes were contradictory to her actions. Tammy's mother made a potentially encouraging statement about her daughter's capability, but the words had little meaning, since her helping her daughter contradicted the words.

Words are often not needed, for they do not contribute anything positive to behavior change. Mother should have made the statement and then re-mained out of the situation to make her words and actions support each other. Tammy's mother's initial statement was intended to foster independence, but her actions actually fostered dependency in Tammy, but only when the actions support the initial words will Tammy move toward independence and self-reliance.

When mother picked Brian up after school, she encountered resistance from her son. He cried because he wanted to stay and play with his friends. Mother tried to reason with Brian by explaining that she had to go home to prepare dinner. She even tried to explain that he had friends at home with whom he could play. He continued to cry. Mother began to get angry but attempted to think of a logical consequence to Brian's defiance. She told Brian that either he'd have to come home now or choose to stay at school. Brian immediately turned and ran back into the building to play with his friends. Mother could not understand why the logical consequence didn't work the way she planned.

Brian didn't go home with mother because the logical consequence was incorrectly established.

We have all tried at some point to reason with our children. Reasoning is an adult's way of trying to show a parent's concern and generally inform the child of the parent's rationale. By reasoning parents *hope* to get the desired result without taking any action. Reasoning logically would be good, except for one "small" problem. Children have their own system of logic, often referred to as "private logic." The private logic of children is often in conflict with the logical reasoning of parents. A mother told her son that he could not have a cookie because it would spoil his dinner. The child understood what his mother said, smiled, and, as his mother walked away, reached for one of the cookies. Mother attempted to use her logical reasoning to communicate how she wanted him to act, but his private logic said, "I want one."

Since logic and reasoning often do not work, actions communicating this logical reasoning need to be demonstrated to children if the reasoning is to have any effect upon their private logic. Only through parental action will children begin to learn what the needs of the situation are and begin to modify their private logic to deal with reality.

The logical consequence planned by Brian's mother backfired and allowed Brian to do what he wanted to do. Brian's mother made a common mistake. The purpose of the misbehavior must be analyzed before the consequence is developed. Brian's mother failed to realize that her son's mistaken goal was power. As stated in chapter 9, logical consequences need to be cautiously used with power-oriented children. They want to do what they choose, when they choose. Logical consequences give children choices, and in Brian's case, one of the choices was what Brian wanted to do in the first place—stay and play at school. Since Brian had to go home, the choice of going or staying should not have been given. He should have been given the choice of *how* he was to go.

Many such situations are actually power struggles. This can be seen in the case of the child who says she doesn't want to go to school one day. This child must be given a choice, told what action the parents will take. We cannot make our children do what we want them to; we can only state what our action will be.

Brian's mother could have told him that if he chose not to come on his own, she would have to carry him. Mother's course of action would therefore have been determined by how the child responded to the choice given. If he chose not to come, she would have had to go into the school and remove him to give her words meaning. Power-oriented children will often test their parents to see how far they can go and still remain in control. The more parents allow their children to get away with, the more they teach them not to listen.

Eric is a seven-year-old brain-damaged child who attended special classes at school. Although he had many learning problems, he progressed at a favorable rate. Eric's biggest problem both at school and at home was his violent temper tantrums and acts of revenge whenever things didn't go the way he wanted them to. The parents were very conscious of trying to avoid these outbursts. They met with some success because they let Eric do what he wanted as a means of avoiding conflict. As Eric got older, they had more difficulty trying to control his violent outbursts. One evening when Eric's father called him in from the backyard for dinner, Eric began throwing one of his tantrums and refused to come. The father tried to calm him down and get him to come to dinner. They had tried this approach many times with virtually no change in Eric's behavior. After his father tried for a few minutes to get him to come in, Eric began to kick his father. His father tried to continue reasoning with Eric, but the kicking continued.

In such obvious power struggles, words are ineffective. They act more as catalysts than as modifiers of the problem. In power struggles involving violent outbursts words do not and cannot set the boundaries for acceptable behavior in our children. Parental actions should set them and should be the means of communicating them. Eric's father needed to stop talking and gently but firmly restrain Eric from kicking. By this action he would have taught Eric that his behavior would not be tolerated. After holding him for a few seconds the father might have released Eric, and if Eric resumed the kicking, the father should have continued to restrain him until the outburst ended. When he finally released him, the father could gently take Eric's hand and lead him to dinner. Eric would learn much sooner what the boundaries of acceptable behavior were if continual parental action of this type were consistently demonstrated in other conflict.

Not all power struggles involve violent behavior, but they may be equally upsetting to the parents. They, too, require parental action instead of words. Parents who do not take action and utilize only words with their children wind up having *parent deaf* children who "tune them out" by mentally blocking their ears. We can be assured of having developed parent deafness in our children when we find ourselves repeating statements with little or no response from them. We need to stop using words and initiate logical actions that fit the needs of the situation. Kicking Eric back, for example, would not have met the needs of the situation, but restraining him would be logical and appropriate.

One of the most difficult lessons for parents to learn is that of keeping their mouths shut during conflict. Even when parents know their words are ineffective, they find it difficult not to talk. When children throw food on the floor, parents respond by verbal reprimands and threats. Parents often talk when they are not sure of the appropriate action. If they stop themselves from verbally responding quickly and repeatedly, they might then be able to come up with an appropriate action for the situation. A logical and appropriate parental action related to the food-throwing incident is to remove the remaining food. The child will soon realize that food throwing means no food until next mealtime. This action communicates to the child that if he is going to be at the table, he needs to conduct himself in a "reasonable" manner.

Words are the weapons in the war between parents and children. Parents should limit their use of negative statements. Parents enhance the probability of developing a mutually respectful relationship through the use of appropriate parental actions.

15

THE BATHROOM TECHNIQUE:
A Lesson in Positive Withdrawal

The technique that many parents believe the most beneficial in redirecting various misbehaviors is the bathroom technique. It is practical and logical to implement.

Mary Elaine is the mother of two children, Rosemary, age three, and Stan, age four; Stan is physically handicapped. She recently contacted a local family counselor to help with problems she was experiencing with her children. Mary Elaine described herself as being at "her wits' end." An extensive evaluation of the problem revealed the children's lack of respect for their mother and what she said: The children controlled the mother. The counselor recommended the bathroom technique.

The next day mother was busily preparing lunch for the children. The children were fighting and demanding food. They were constantly getting in their mother's way, which made it almost impossible for mother to remain calm. Rather than yelling, as she would have done in the past, she decided to take the parental action recommended. Mary Elaine said that if the children could not behave in a reasonable manner, she would not be able to remain in the kitchen. As in the past the children exhibited "parent deafness" and continued their disruptive behavior. Mother stopped her activities and told the children that when they could act in a reasonable manner, she would be back to finish preparing lunch. Mother removed herself from the situation and went into the bathroom, which she had amply stocked with reading materials.

The children waited for a few seconds to see what mother was going to do. When she did not come out of the bathroom, they began yelling for her. When mother did not respond and remained in the bathroom, Stan began kicking the door with his feet. Mother thought she was going to lose her mind from the kicking and yelling during the first ten minutes. Although it was difficult, she knew she must remain calm. If she gave in to her children's demands at this point, it would be much more difficult to implement corrective measures the next time. It seemed like an eternity to mother until the kicking and yelling stopped. At this point mother opened the door to the bathroom and stepped over her son, who was lying on the floor. As she walked toward the kitchen, she saw her daughter, Rosemary, with a number of her mother's favorite record albums. They were covered with sugar. In a state of internal rage mother very calmly went over to her daughter and without saying a word picked up the albums and took them into the kitchen. She dusted them off and put them into their jackets. She then finished making lunch for the children. The children remained very quiet, sitting on the living room floor.

Note that Mary Elaine's removal to the bathroom was not a spontaneous or haphazardly planned action. Any time parents plan to remove themselves from the visual supervision of their children, their children's safety needs to become a major consideration in that action. Because of the many hazards that can befall children, planned precautions need to be taken to minimize *any* potential injury. Consider the child's age, intellectual and physical limitations, and the general physical surroundings in which the act of withdrawal will be carried out.

The bathroom technique was the way Mary Elaine escaped the stress and demands of her children. The bathroom is one of the few places in the home that is private. The bathroom can be much more easily tolerated if there is something to do—Mary Elaine had reading material available. Other parents have found that taking a relaxing bath, having a radio available, cleaning the bathroom, or having a copy of this book in the bathroom to read helps them to remain calm and under control.

The effectiveness of this technique comes from the parents' ability to follow through with an action. This action allows the parent the opportunity to remain calm by not being in the presence of the misbehavior, and it also communicates to the child that the parent will not tolerate the misbehavior.

Many children misbehave to get attention or power, which requires involvement by the parents or other adults, and the withdrawal of the adult does not feed into these mistaken goals. This communicates to children that the parents will respond to them when they choose to demonstrate more cooperative behaviors.

It is apparent that the outcome of Mary Elaine's situation was positive. If she had given in when disturbing behavior increased, she would have accomplished nothing. Rosemary and Stan would have believed that even though mother ran to the bathroom, increased misbehavior would get them what they want. If mother had come out of the bathroom before the children calmed down, control of the situation would be back in the children's hands.

Gordon was instructed to use the bathroom technique when his daughter made excessive demands and threw temper tantrums when she didn't get what she wanted. One evening his daughter began pounding on the table where they were sitting. Gordon immediately removed himself to the bathroom to give his daughter time to calm down. While he was in the bathroom, Gordon heard his daughter running through the house slamming the doors so hard he could feel the vibrations. He immediately came out of the bathroom and spanked her for her unacceptable behavior.

The daughter found her father's limits. This situation brings up a major concern of many mothers and fathers. Remaining in the bathroom gives the appearance of not taking any action and therefore of allowing children to do whatever they please. The removal of oneself from a situation is often thought of as giving up or giving in to children. However, it is a positive therapeutic technique: By withdrawing from a misbehavior, you in fact remain in control of yourself, and you do not feed into the mistaken goal of your children. Once we give in to children's negative behavior, we lose control of the situation. We respond to the misbehavior the way they want. The bathroom technique allows parents the *choice* of being able to remain in control of themselves or give up the control to their children.

It is sometimes difficult for parents to remain in the bathroom until their children quiet down. The difficulty usually arises when parents hear their children crying or when it sounds like one child is "killing" the other one. The breaking point for many parents is often the sound of glass breaking or hearing every door in the house being slammed. Children will resort to the physical damage of property, hoping to bring mother or father running out of the bathroom. These are difficult times, but training our children is not a simple task. When you decide to use the bathroom technique, be prepared to stay in the bathroom until *you* decide it is the proper time to leave, not when your children "smoke" you out by their ingenious tactics. There are two steps one can take to make these difficult times more bearable. First, parents should prepare the house ahead of time. Remove any objects which are valuable, easily damaged, or potentially dangerous. This will help put your mind at ease. The second step is to develop a consequence for the misbehavior that occurs while you're in the bathroom. Remember to remain calm and firm. Running out of the bathroom upset is exactly what you should avoid. It will in no way benefit the relationship with your children, but will only show them just how far they must go to get you to respond the way they want.

16

AVOID REINFORCING NEGATIVE BEHAVIOR

HOW PARENTS CAN PERPETUATE MISBEHAVIOR

Various misbehaviors in exceptional children develop because of the parents' initial reaction to the behavior. Parents accidentally maintain many unwanted misbehaviors through their reaction to them. Attempts to diminish the misbehavior may in fact serve to encourage it.

All behavior has a purpose, and the parents' first reaction to the misbehavior usually feeds into the child's purpose. That first reaction of a shouted "No," "Stop it," "What are you doing?" is often exactly how the child hoped you would respond. She received the parents' attention and involvement.

Chad was playing in the kitchen while mother was preparing dinner. As mother busily worked, Chad began to bang the cabinet door into the wall of their house trailer. The sound echoed throughout the house. Mother was initially startled by the banging. She quickly turned around and saw Chad banging the door. She turned and yelled at Chad, "Stop that!" Her reaction helped guarantee that the misbehavior would occur again.

Chad's mother did not take the time to understand the purpose of the misbehavior. She failed to utilize the awareness of her emotional reaction of

92

irritation to understand the misbehavior. Instead, she allowed her emotional reaction to control her behavior toward Chad, and she reprimanded him, guaranteeing the fulfillment of Chad's mistaken goal of undue attention. Chad did not stop his negative behavior because he was seeking mother's attention and he got it.

Parents consciously need to be aware of the effect of allowing their emotional reactions such as irritation, anger, hurt, or despair to control them. They should utilize these emotional reactions to understand the child's mistaken goal. In this way parents can redirect the child's unconstructive behaviors instead of accidentally feeding into them. As Chad succeeds in getting mother to respond to his need for undue attention, they find themselves locked into an endless pattern of reinforcing each other's negative behavior. This cyclical pattern leaves little room for the potential development of positive behavior.

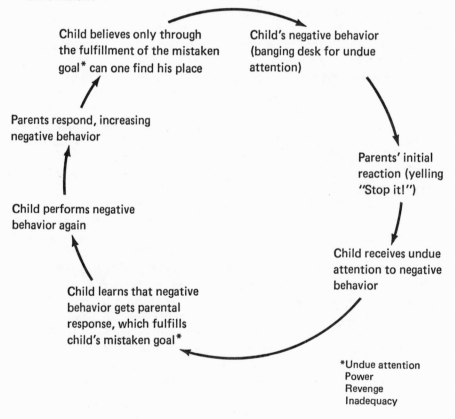

This cycle shows the cause-effect relationship between the parents' lack of understanding of why children misbehave and the parents' ineffective disciplinary methods. Parents mistakenly confirm children's belief that they can only find their place and fulfill their goals through negative behaviors.

Jane's mother has been working closely with the school to develop her daughter's ability to put her shoes on by herself. At school the teachers reported great success. At home it was a different story. Jane appeared to get very frustrated whenever she was asked to put on her own shoes. She would cry and plead with mom and dad to help her. Jane's parents attempted to encourage her by telling her she was able to do it by herself. After a time, as her crying persisted, they gave in and helped her. One day mother noticed Jane taking off her shoes, carrying them in the house, and asking for assistance to put them on. Mother was amazed at how Jane was able to get the family so involved in this situation. She finally realized what a good attention-getting device Jane had devised with nobody the wiser.

Ignoring Jane's crying and whining appeared to be the most logical way to communicate to Jane that her unproductive behavior would not command the attention she thought it would. Mother and father agreed to ignore this attention-getting behavior to get Jane to take care of herself and become more independent. Whenever the crying or pleading occurred, mother ignored it and did not help her with her shoes. After this persisted for some time, mother would tell Jane that she was not going to get any help and would have to do it by herself. As Jane's crying increased, so did mother's frustration. She began to tell Jane that she knew she could do it by herself and that there's no way she would do it for her.

In mother's attempt to ignore the misbehavior, the situation actually began to develop into a power struggle between Jane and her mother. Although mother had the right intentions, she did not understand how to ignore *totally*. She thought that if she did not feed into the whims and do it for her, that that would be sufficient, but ignoring is a more complicated procedure. It involves the total removal of parental involvement. Although Jane's mother did not put on her daughter's shoes, she did give attention by reminding her many times that she was not going to do it for her. This had the same effect of reinforcing the undesirable behavior. Along with the numerous reminders, mother's tone of voice grew more intense and irritated, communicating continued parental involvement. If she were *truly* to ignore the misbehavior, she should have remained silent about the shoes. She should not have reminded

Jane that she would have to put on her own shoes. If mother wanted to inform Jane once that she would have to take care of her own shoes, she should still monitor her tone of voice carefully to keep from communicating any sense of displeasure or irritation. That may be just enough attention to encourage the misbehavior. That is why the situation between Jane and her mother developed into a power struggle.

Ignoring is not easy. It involves a multitude of verbal and nonverbal components. We've all been confronted with statements people have made to us where the words say one thing, but how they are said means another. "I've never *seen* an outfit like that before" may verbally be communicating a positive concept such as you're a fashion pace-setter. "I've never seen an outfit like *that* before" may communicate a totally different meaning. What is really being said is that the speaker doesn't like the outfit. We need to be aware that irritation or anger can be communicated through our tone of voice and conscious monitoring is the only way to control it.

Nonverbal factors such as body language, facial expressions, and eye contact, are but a few of the ways individuals communicate. The process of ignoring necessitates our awareness of these areas of communication. Are you really ignoring your child's temper tantrum as you bang pots and pans around the kitchen in irritation? Are you ignoring when your facial expression communicates, "If you do that one more time . . . ?" Are you truly removed from the situation when your eyes follow all your child's disruptive behaviors? All these nonverbal behaviors have the same potential of feeding into misbehavior as your verbal and immediate physical involvement. To practice the principle of parental ignoring requires the ability to interpret all those factors that may have the effect of indicating unnecessary involvement with your child's misbehavior.

Some of our children's goals in misbehaving may require a different type of ignoring. When Steve is hanging and tugging on your leg because his demands are not being met, it may be physically and emotionally difficult to remain in the same room while you attempt to ignore the misbehavior. Attempting to feed the baby while you drag Steve around the room on your leg may become more than your patience can handle. Your physical presence alone may be enough to maintain Steve's undesirable behavior. As long as you remain in the room, Steve can hope that his misbehavior will evoke the desired payoff. To communicate to Steve that there is no such hope, you must remove yourself from him. In a case like this you can use the bathroom technique, explained in the previous chapter.

SAFETY PRECAUTIONS

Parents of exceptional children are often confronted with situations like Tom's head banging (see chapter 12). His action created an almost intolerable situation. The most effective method of diminishing the misbehavior is ignoring. Exceptional children may exhibit many behaviors that parents need to ignore if they are to be extinguished. However, the nature of some behaviors, like Tom's head banging, makes them difficult to ignore. Because of possible physical injury to the child, it becomes emotionally trying for parents to ignore these behaviors. Parents of exceptional children are caught in a double bind: Ignoring is contradictory to past levels of involvement because of a feeling that special assistance is required. Even knowing that ignoring may be one of the most positive techniques for diminishing negative behavior, many parents find it difficult to make a decision. Certainly precautions need to be taken, for the safety of the child as well as others around him. A main consideration in any remedial procedure is the safety of the children; thought should be given as to the possible outcomes before any remedial procedures are undertaken.

For example, safety precautions were mandatory to protect Tom from any possible physical injury as a result of his head banging. His parents put a helmet on his head to lessen the impact of the banging, a necessary precaution before the parents could ignore him. The child's environment should also be considered. Potentially harmful materials such as knives, breakable objects, and things cooking on the stove should be removed. It is easy for many situations, no matter how big or how small, to get out of hand if these simple precautions are not taken. Once they are taken, a parent is able to focus directly on the specific unwanted behavior. This allows a greater probability that the remedial procedure will be successful.

ENCOURAGING THE POSITIVE WHILE
MINIMIZING THE NEGATIVE

The success experienced by Tom's parents can be attributed not only to their ability to avoid reinforcing the negative behavior through ignoring but also to their ability to increase more acceptable behavior in Tom. This was accomplished by giving recognition through actions to Tom for his positive behavior. There should be no recognition for his negative behavior. Whenever Tom stopped banging his head, his parents would return to the room expressing positive facial expressions and communicating encouraging statements in a pleasant tone of voice. They also expressed their pleasure with his increased ability to restrain himself from banging his head by touching and holding him. Tom soon began to demonstrate positive behavior, which generated more positive recognition from his parents.

Minimizing negative behaviors by not giving recognition to them goes hand in hand with encouragement. This principle is amply demonstrated by the teacher who frantically called the school psychologist. She reported that one of the boys in her special class was masturbating. The psychologist responded almost immediately by going to the classroom to observe the situation and to ask the teacher some basic questions so as to fully understand the difficulty. The psychologist asked the teacher how many times she had observed the child masturbating in class. To the amazement of the psychologist, she said she had seen it only this once.

The saying "Don't make a mountain out of a molehill" seems to describe best the principle of minimizing the negative. The more emphasis the teacher and the psychologist put on the situation, the greater the potential for developing a misbehavior that is otherwise relatively nonexistent. Giving positive recognition for positive behavior needs to be coordinated with an equal effort to minimize the recognition given for many negative behaviors children will test out. The more conscious we are of minimizing our reactions to negative behaviors, which occur in all exceptional children, the greater the potential for our success in not reinforcing them.

DOING THE OPPOSITE

There are numerous principles for parents to follow in avoiding reinforcing negative behaviors in their children. One principle for parents to be aware of might be termed "doing the opposite." As parents understand their children's goals and how they as parents have been perpetuating these, they will learn to react in a manner opposite from what their children expect.

The week following a meeting for parents of crippled children, which focused on avoiding the reinforcement of negative behaviors, Mrs. White reported a difficulty she had solved since the last meeting. Her son Justin had been giving her fits when she attempted to give him a bath. He would go to his room, lock the door, and not come out. His mother would plead and coax him to come out to take his bath before bed. This ritual lasted about one-half hour. It totally aggravated his mother.

After Mrs. White thought about the group's discussion on avoiding the reinforcement of negative behaviors by doing the opposite, she realized that her pleading and coaxing were only continuing the misbehavior. Since his behavior was for undue attention, she realized that by doing the opposite, she might not feed into the attention-getting behavior. Instead of standing by the door pleading with Justin, mother simply informed him that if he wanted to stay in his room, that was his choice, but whenever he wanted to take his bath, she would be glad to help him. At this point mother walked away from the door and went about her own business. Mother first understood that Justin's mistaken goal was undue attention. She then figured out that by doing the opposite of how she usually responded, she could effectively eliminate the misbehavior. Before parents attempt to diminish negative behaviors by doing the opposite, they must first analyze the situation and the child's mistaken goal to make sure that their new response has the effect of extinguishing and not reinforcing.

Parents unintentionally reinforce negative behaviors in their children. Much of the parents' effort to diminish certain misbehavior goes unnoticed because children capitalize on unintentional reinforcement of their negative behaviors. As parents implement systematic corrective procedures for diminishing unwanted behavior in their children, they still need to maintain an overall awareness of their parent-child relationship. If parents can avoid reinforcing negative behaviors—without concerning themselves with corrective methods— they will have advanced halfway toward eliminating unwanted behaviors.

Positive Parental Attitude

17

GOOD PARENTS ARE ALLOWED TO SAY NO

Anna is a young girl who has taken a variety of medications to help control a severe seizure problem. Although the seizures are controlled to some degree, they are not cured. Because of the various hardships Anna's mother has seen her endure, she makes every effort to lessen life's frustrations for her. In recent months Anna has made some unreasonable demands on her parents. The parents know they should not give in to Anna's demands, for her own good. But they do not want to add any additional frustration to their daughter's life at this time so they give in to her undue demands. The intensity of Anna's demands has become increasingly greater as she senses her parents' desire to eliminate her frustration.

Because of physiological conditions Anna must make various modifications in her life-style. Her parents feel guilty about this; consequently they try to eliminate *all* other frustrations in her life. But her parents cannot guarantee they will be around forever to eliminate frustrations for her—eventually she will have to cope. By continually giving in and not saying no when the child places undue demands upon them, the parents allow themselves to be placed in a subservient role to their child. The child develops a self-centered life-style.

Fulfilling every whim and every demand of children is not a necessary condition of being a good parent. Good parents are allowed to say no. It is a common difficulty for parents to stick to their words when they tell their children they cannot do something or have something. Parents feel that it is part of being a "good parent" to make it as pleasant for their children as possible by granting them their desires. Most parents want to be good parents. Yet there is confusion as to how this can be achieved. Many parents try to be "good" by trying to make their children happy and free of any stress or frustration. Most parents consciously believe this to be impossible, but their inability to say no is nonetheless evidence of a futile attempt to achieve a frustration-free life-style for their children. Good parents are those who attempt to teach their children constructive means of finding their place by developing constructive coping mechanisms to deal with life's frustrations.

Taken to an extreme, wanting to be a good parent is often referred to as the "good parent syndrome." Anna's mother demonstrates how readily this syndrome occurs in parents of exceptional children. The parents may feel bad because their child has many limitations in life. By saying no they would only add to the already existing limitations. The parents may feel they are the only ones really to understand their child. This gives them the right to give in to their child's demands. They view this as being "necessary" for the child's well-being. These as well as other rationalizations may be given by parents of exceptional children to justify their inability to say no. Parents ought to monitor these rationalizations to see what the true effects of not saying no are upon themselves and their children. The following chart illustrates the effects of the parents' ability and inability to say no.

Parents' Inability to Say No	*Parents' Ability to Say No*
Promotes self-centeredness in children	Helps children develop social interest
Promotes more violent outbursts in children	Helps children decrease their violent outbursts
Promotes little sense of value for property in children	Helps children develop a sense of value for property
Promotes a sense of irresponsibility in children	Helps children develop a sense of responsibility
Promotes an inability to cope with lifes's frustrations in children	Helps children learn to cope with life's frustrations
Promotes a feeling of uncooperativeness in children	Helps children develop a sense of cooperation with others

Promotes a temporary false harmony with children	Helps develop long-term harmonious relationships with children
Promotes a lack of self-respect in parents	Helps parents develop respect for their own needs
Promotes a servile attitude in parents	Helps parents develop a cooperative attitude
Promotes a martyr syndrome in parents	Helps parents feel OK even when children exhibit frustrations

Michael is an only child who was born with one arm. His parents are highly protective and provide him with a great deal of assistance to help him overcome his handicap. All family activities revolve around Michael. There is very little that he wants that he doesn't get. The word no rarely appears in conversations between Michael and his parents. Without Michael even requesting or demanding something, his parents will attempt to give him what they think he will like and make him happy. On occasions where other prople receive gifts, such as his mother's birthday, Michael will also receive a gift. They don't want him to feel left out. When his parents go shopping, they make it a point to bring some small gift home to him. Michael always receives special consideration from his parents.

Although Michael gets extremely excited when he receives gifts, he rarely ever plays with them after the first day. He shows little concern for the care of his toys. It is not unusual for him to tell his parents the following day that he has lost or broken his new toys.

The effect of his parents' inability to say no has begun to create a self-centered attitude within Michael. He has begun to see life as a situation where he counts only when others serve his wishes. Michael is not truly conscious of this belief. Yet his actions clearly demonstrate how strongly he believes the world *should* revolve around him. His sadness when he does not receive special treatment illustrates his self-centeredness. Michael is a pampered child. He is unable to take no for an answer. He cannot deal with life's many disappointments. By never saying no to any of his demands or wishes, his parents only create a temporary harmony in the family. They shirk the responsibility of being good parents by not teaching Michael that there are limits in life. Michael's parents erroneously believe that they are winning the battles, but they will soon discover they have lost the war. When Michael faces reality, he will lack the essential skills necessary for coping with life's frustrations.

Many parents wonder why their children want something so badly, yet when they receive it they show little care for the object. Irresponsibility and lack of sense of value for property are by-products of a pampered life-style created in children by their parents' never saying no. When children get everything they want, they do not learn to appreciate what they have. The regularity of parents giving in and their inability to say no need to be realistically modified. Children do not learn a sense of value for property when their parents immediately replace their broken or lost toys. If there is no limit to what our children demand, they illogically distort the value of material objects and the seemingly limitless supply of money. Children do not become responsible because their parents tell them they should. Responsibility can only be taught through parental actions.

Sheila was experiencing difficulty with the neighborhood children. She ran home when things didn't go well with the other children. It was difficult for Sheila to work out difficulties between herself and her friends. She was uncooperative and demanding. She always wanted whatever someone had. She preferred playing with children considerably younger than herself or with adults. This allowed her to control the others.

The inability of Sheila's parents to say no to her had a profound effect upon her ability to cooperate in the give-and-take among friends. Sheila was so used to having things always go her way at home that she began to believe that this is the way she should be treated by everyone. It's no wonder that she was attracted to playing with little children. She was able to control the group and do just what she wanted with little resistance. Situations where cooperativeness is required creates inner tension for children who have always had things go their way.

Human relationships, especially those with peers, will at some time require cooperation. Children must learn they cannot have all their demands met by others. This is taught by parents through their ability to say no. The children find it much easier to form healthier relationships when they are able to cooperate.

Take the child who demands the candy that is strategically placed at the store's checkout counter and has a violent outburst of temper and anger when the father initially says no. This child, like many others, is so used to getting what he wants that he exhibits violent and disruptive behaviors until his demands are met. These violent outbursts would not occur if he had learned that he was just wasting energy. However, parents usually give in to their children's demands when they are blackmailed by violent outbursts, especially in public. Not only do these violent outbursts work, but they are also a graphic representation of the extent to which children believe they should get what they want. Actions speak louder than words. Saying no has no meaning until it is supported by parental actions. The sooner parents are able to say no to their children, the better able the children will be to deal with the many frustrations of life.

When we enter one of our favorite restaurants, we expect to receive a particular type of service. We expect to be served promptly. We expect excellent food, and we expect it to be prepared the way we want it. The parents' inability to say no causes their child to expect that same type of service in the home. She believes her parents' only function is to meet her demands. She expects her parents to be servants to her. Parents playing this role show a lack of their respect for themselves. They fail to fulfill their own needs and become the victims of their children's tyranny.

The desire to be a good parent, and to assist children in meeting life's tasks to the best of their ability, is a goal of most parents. It gives a great deal of satisfaction to help children through difficulties while making life as pleasant as possible. However, this is not to say that good parents cannot refuse to give in to some of their children's demands or desires. When parents can say no, they help their children make life more pleasant by teaching them to deal effectively with life's demands and limits.

18

CHILDREN'S GREATEST HANDICAP: OVERPROTECTION

Bernie, age six, was born with a congenital heart defect that requires modification of his physical activity. Although there is a public school nearby that can provide adaptive physical education for Bernie, his parents decided to send him to a private school that would monitor all his activities. Because the school has a physician on call at all times, they felt the private school was a good choice.

Bernie enjoys playing outside and often requests permission to go to the local community playground. Although Bernie's parents know that he enjoys going to the playground, they usually will not let him go unless they accompany him and monitor his exertion level. Every morning Bernie walks to the end of the block to catch the private-school bus. His mother watches from an upstairs window to make sure he does not run and that he gets there safely. Mother insists that Bernie walk on the left-hand sidewalk of the road because she cannot observe him from the right-hand one. When Bernie is home playing outside the house, mother rarely does any work. She goes from window to window trying to keep constant track of his activity level. At the first sign of any exertion, mother goes to the door and reminds Bernie that he needs to watch himself.

Bernie's parents want to protect and assist their son. This is natural and understandable. However, it is the responsibility of parents to teach and to train their children to cope with life effectively. No parent can control life either for himself or for his children. The futile attempt to do so will only lead to the opposite of what all parents hope to accomplish through their overprotection. Rather than teaching effective methods of coping with life, overprotection inhibits the development of life-coping skills. Parents give so much of their life, time, and energy to *do* for their children rather than to *teach* them. Since they do all the coping and thinking for their children, the children see no need to learn to do for themselves.

REASONS PARENTS OVERPROTECT

When we try to be good parents, especially of an exceptional child, over-protecting is a natural pitfall. To move toward being the best parents we can be, we must understand the development of overprotection.

One of the main reasons parents overprotect is that they see physiological conditions limiting their children. Often parents overprotect and exaggerate their children's basic limitations by not allowing any activity or exertion. Bernie does have certain limits, but his parents exaggerate these limits by stifling any physical activity.

A second reason for overprotecting is the parents' fictitious belief that they always know what is best for their children. This belief maintains the children's dependency and their feelings of helplessness. By placing children in a dependent role, parents establish themselves in a position of superiority and power. This sense of superiority is then enhanced by the continuing evolution of the dependent relationship. The more dependent children become, the more they need their parents. The more they need their parents, the more powerful and more superior the parents feel. Although it is done in the context of trying to help and for the "well-being" of their children, over-protecting only serves to maintain the parents' superior position and their children's dependency.

The third reason parents overprotect is because they feel guilty. Parents of a handicapped child may subconsciously feel that they caused their child's handicap. Because of this feeling parents overcompensate, overprotect, and smother their child.

The fourth possible cause of parental overprotection is the feeling of rejection on the part of the parents toward their children. Parents are often afraid to admit to these thoughts of rejection, and they compensate by over-protecting. Since the feeling of rejecting their own flesh and blood is so socially unacceptable, parents move to the most opposite extreme from rejection, which is overprotection. A statement symptomatic of this attitude is the resentful question, "What did I do to deserve this?" Many exceptional children radically change their parents' life-styles, limiting their activities and creating extra responsibilities. Resenting the child is not uncommon. The parents hope effectively to overcome these personally unacceptable feelings by overprotecting. However, they will find that this cannot be accomplished, because overprotection makes the child more dependent on the parents, creating additional responsibilities and burdens.

Parents should also be aware of the danger of a subtle, yet highly debilitating method of overprotection. Mothers and fathers of a handicapped child may go to extremes to protect the child from what they view as the negative impact of the handicap itself. They use deception and the "white" lie as a means of hiding from the child basic realities about his dysfunction. This overprotection serves to maintain parental control and to make sure the child "never" experiences the handicap. But parents cannot keep their children in the dark forever. Sooner or later the child will have to learn about his disability and assume responsibility for his own care. It may not be easy to explain the disability and its effects to a young child, but parenting has its difficult moments. Explaining a child's condition to him in a simple and casual manner will assist him in adjusting to his disability. The disability is the child's, not the parents'. He must learn to deal with it effectively and to live a productive life. Overprotecting will not teach the child to cope effectively. His courage to make progress needs to be fostered and his independence encouraged. This can best be accomplished by parental support and confidence in his ability to cope with his disability.

CHILDREN'S RESPONSES TO OVERPROTECTION

Children may interpret overprotection in many ways. It is closely interrelated with their mistaken goals of misbehavior. Overprotection generally elicits two responses from children. The first response is anger and resentment against the parents. These feelings foster a rebellious pattern of behavior. The parents' attempts to control their child's activities have such a stifling effect that many children break away and react with the opposite behavior. When children react to overprotection in a rebellious manner, no amount of logical reasoning can change the rebellious acts. Parents cannot say, "That's not good for you because you'll get hurt." The child who wants power will do the opposite of what the parents want, even to the point of getting hurt. This sort of logical reasoning by parents only aggravates and perpetuates the rebelliousness.

Bernie's parents will begin to see temper tantrums and more rebellious outbursts. The increase in rebelliousness is often accompanied by an increase in anger against parents and other authority figures. The initial parental concern generates overprotection. Parents are often caught off guard by their child's reaction to their concern. It is difficult for them to understand why Bernie would run across the street or overexert himself at the park. His parents only want what's best for him and want to protect him from injury.

A sense of *inadequacy* is the second and the most debilitating reaction children can have to overprotection. And this sense inevitably becomes incorporated into their life-style as a mistaken goal. Depending on the amount of overprotection, some children grow to feel that they are unable to care for themselves, work out any of their problems, or make their own decisions. They feel totally unable to meet the standards set by adults. Overprotection demonstrates the parents' lack of faith in their children and spawns a lack of self-confidence. Although parents do this to shield their children, overprotection may be more debilitating than the limited physical restraints the disability alone places on their children. Because of his parents' constant monitoring of his behavior both in and out of the house, Bernie could easily develop many fears, phobias, and a general fear of not being able to succeed. This fear of failure keeps him out of the mainstream of life. He believes he can survive only if people do for him and take care of him. Eventually this overprotection will lead to Bernie's becoming discouraged, giving up, and believing himself an incapable individual. It is difficult enough for parents to encourage small steps of progress in an exceptional child without the added difficulty of having to overcome the effects of discouragement in the child.

Whether we overprotect to maintain our own superiority or to protect our children from the realities of their disability, it still leads to the same inevitable conclusion. We unintentionally strip our children of the coping strategies they can learn only from experience in life. Our children do need our assistance, but this assistance should teach them skills for coping with life. We should monitor our own need to overprotect and allow our children to experience their own capabilities while being prepared to lend parental support when needed. In this way we *teach* our children skills for tomorrow, as opposed to *giving* solutions for today.

19

ENCOURAGE INDEPENDENCE

The main responsibility given to all parents of all species, both animal and human, is to develop activities that promote independent living in their offspring. Children find themselves dependent and helpless at birth; they rely upon their parents for everything. At the birth of an infant, his parents take on the responsibility for his total care, but as he moves from infancy to adulthood, his parents' efforts should be to teach and train him to deal independently with life's tasks. His parents can accomplish this development by encouraging his independence.

Most children have the capability to handle the transition from dependent to independent living. Exceptional children, however, may be hampered in the development skills necessary for independent living. Parents of exceptional children may need to spend more time than other parents in encouraging their children toward independent living. The limitations of an exceptional child demand a more consciously planned effort from parents. This is necessary for the child to overcome these limitations and move away from dependence toward the highest level of independent functioning possible.

Terry was a seventeen-year-old, totally blind high school junior who was referred by his high school counselor for vocational and career assessment.

Because of Terry's success in school, he planned to go to college but was unsure about what he wanted to study. An extensive battery of interest, achievement, and aptitude tests, was administered. The analysis of the results produced some startling contradictions. It was assumed that the results would be similar to that of his school records. He had A's and B's in all academic areas, but the test results indicated substantially lower skills. This was most noticeable in Terry's mathematical ability. Although he got a B in basic algebra, he was unable to perform even the simplest of mathematical computations. Terry had always been encouraged to pursue a college education because of his grades and outgoing personality. The rehabilitation counselor was now confronted with the difficult task of going over the results with Terry and his family, disclosing to them that he scored far below the level needed in the majority of areas for potential success in college.

All along Terry thought he was developing skills for independent living. He in fact was "duped" into believing that he was performing at a college entrance level. It is difficult to pass courses such as algebra without being able to do simple addition or subtraction. His parents and teachers all had a part in the problem now facing Terry. In their attempts to help Terry avoid failures, they overlooked his true potential. They assumed that because he was blind, he was incapable of learning the material, and they assumed the responsibility for his happiness by giving him what they thought he wanted and could not achieve on his own—good grades. Feeling sorry for him, they actually took away his chance to develop independence. They let their emotional reaction to Terry cripple him intellectually and psychologically. Instead of putting their energies into helping him overcome his visual limitations, they created an even greater limitation by giving him a false impression of his abilities.

Parents of exceptional children are often sidetracked when developing independence in their children. This occurs because parents pity their children when they see the difficulties with which their children struggle. Although the child who is severely hampered in mobility by the use of leg braces and crutches has often learned to adapt effectively to his situation, people frequently respond with the attitude "Oh, you poor dear." The person does not feel sorry for the particular circumstance that has befallen the child, but rather for the *child*. Empathizing with a child about circumstances that have an adverse effect is a positive acknowledgment that we understand the child's feelings. "Oh, you poor dear" is a negative response, suggesting that the child is incapable of dealing with the situation. Feeling pity for the child does not separate her from the circumstances that have befallen her. This attitude conveys the impression that because certain circumstances create limitations, the child as a person is also limited. Empathizing separates the circumstances from the child. It communicates that although the circumstance presents limitations, the person is not limited as such nor any less equal as a human being.

Consciously avoiding pitying helps encourage independence in our children. Although it may be hard to stop others from responding out of pity, it is the daily empathetic parental responses that will have the most positive effect upon building independence. When we have eliminated pity, the use of encouragement, the avoidance of reinforcing negative behavior, the consistency of corrective measures, and the use of other democratic principles need to be incorporated into a systematic plan. The more independent skills we can develop in our children, the more they can contribute to others.

Dependence and independence follow an initially similar cyclical pattern. The following diagrams illustrate both the cycles and their potential outcomes for children.

Dependent Outcomes	*Independent Outcomes*
Diminishes resourcefulness	Increases problem-solving ability
Child lacks courage to face life's tasks	Child gains courage to face life's tasks
Gets others to feel sorry	Promotes healthy relationships
Puts others into child's service	Creates more cooperative behavior
Gets angry when things aren't done by others	Promotes more positive feelings
Feels not OK	Feels OK

We need to analyze the cycles carefully and ask ourselves which one we want for our children. It becomes obvious upon close analysis which cycle gives our children the greatest benefits. It is clear that the independent cycle provides long-term benefits for ourselves and our children. The dependent cycle results in the efforts of others to do more for our children, rather than teaching our children to be self-sufficient. Parents need to consider more than just their children's immediate needs if independence for their children is a primary goal. Thinking of future needs and the kinds of skills children need to live in the least restrictive environment is central to the long-range

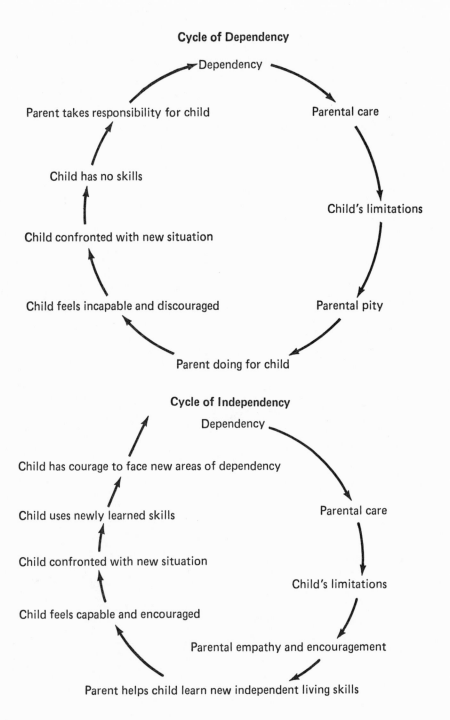

Cycle of Dependency

Dependency

Parent takes responsibility for child

Parental care

Child has no skills

Child's limitations

Child confronted with new situation

Child feels incapable and discouraged

Parental pity

Parent doing for child

Cycle of Independency

Dependency

Child has courage to face new areas of dependency

Parental care

Child uses newly learned skills

Child confronted with new situation

Child's limitations

Child feels capable and encouraged

Parental empathy and encouragement

Parent helps child learn new independent living skills

planning needed for exceptional children. This future planning is imperative, since we will not be there when our children live their future. We need to prepare for that day, to equip our children with the tools to build a life for themselves. Independence is the tool we can give that will allow our children to carve out their own futures to the best of their ability.

20

HOW TO COMMUNICATE WITH YOUR CHILDREN

*I know you think you heard what I said, but is
what you heard what I really meant?*

At first glance the above quote may appear confusing, but if we think about what the words are saying, the message becomes quite clear. Often we think we are communicating a message, but to our dismay a totally different message had been perceived. It is frustrating to have a conversation with someone and feel as though two totally different conversations are going on at the same time. Knowing how to communicate is the catalyst for all effective human interactions, and that is especially true of parent-child interactions. The role of parents is to influence and guide their children in the development of certain values and behaviors. Parents must effectively communicate to achieve what is most beneficial for their children.

At a parent study group meeting for parents of exceptional children, Mr. Adams asked for some assistance in handling a problem involving his daughter Lisa's impending report card. The day before, he had received a phone call from Lisa's teacher informing him that his daughter was failing almost all her subjects. The teacher thought he ought to be forewarned of the situation. The group attempted to help Mr. Adams deal with his frustration and plan how to handle the situation most effectively when Lisa brought home the report card. The group focused on how Mr. Adams could communicate encouragement and help Lisa become more productive in school. The group got Mr. Adams to practice various statements that would focus on something positive about Lisa's schoolwork even though he knew she was going to receive a number of F's. Although he was still frustrated, Mr. Adams felt much more adequately prepared to talk to his daughter when she brought her report card home. The following week Mr. Adams told the group what happened.

(Lisa, with head bowed, asks dad to look and sign the report card.)

MR. ADAMS: How do you feel about it?

LISA: Not real good.

MR. ADAMS: Well, it looks like you really put a lot of effort into your art class (encouraging statement).

LISA   (with deep feeling): I put a lot of effort into my other subjects also.

MR. ADAMS   (voice raised): You couldn't tell by looking at your *grades*.

(Lisa is silent, with eyes brimming.)

Mr. Adams knew what he wanted to communicate, but the final message given to Lisa was not what he intended. He wanted to focus on Lisa's accomplishments, building on those to achieve the most beneficial results for Lisa. Although he knew this and began to encourage her by his initial statement, his final message communicated not the encouragement, but his total frustration and annoyance with Lisa. The effect of Mr. Adams's initial encouraging statement was lessened by his final message, which was devastating to Lisa. This becomes obvious when we look at Lisa's response.

The situation emphasizes the importance of communication between parents and children. If Mr. Adams wanted Lisa to succeed in school and to value her education, his communication would have had to relay this message. Instead, he communicated to Lisa his displeasure with her and her poor performance. Any satisfaction she might have felt with the things she learned was taken away.

Any healthy, positive relationship relies upon mutual respect between two individuals. Nagging, being critical, or putting the other person down does not allow a mutually respectful relationship to develop. If our responsibility is to influence our children positively, a healthy relationship is mandatory. Through proper communication this relationship can be developed and sustained.

Communication between parents and children is a two-way street. Being able to communicate a particular message accurately to other people means having them listen and understand what you tried to communicate. Communicating a positive message, however, also means that we effectively avoid giving a double meaning to our words or actions.

The communication of a particular message is transmitted in two distinct ways to children, verbal or nonverbal. We can communicate to a child that we care either by saying directly to the child that we love him or by demonstrating our love through a physical gesture such as a hug or kiss. Both communicate a message of affection from the parent to the child. The problem with much of the communication between parents and children is that children misinterpret the parents' message. This is especially true when disciplinary action is involved.

VERBAL COMMUNICATION

Usually when they discipline their children, parents place themselves in a superior position. This leads to ineffective communication, for they tend to discipline by nagging, threatening, arguing, demanding, and various other authoritative methods of controlling the child. Any chance for effective communication between the parent and child is stifled.

Democratic methods of discipline allow parents to communicate with their children on a more equal basis. Communicating on an equal basis helps generate cooperativeness and mutual respect, and it increases the child's feelings of self-worth. The authoritative methods of communication serve to maintain parental superiority, keeping the child in an inferior position. This develops rebelliousness, resentment, and dependency in the child. The parents are unable to communicate what they want to communicate, and the child is unable to listen to what her parents are trying to say.

This type of communication can be easily seen when it is graphically represented.

This is a model of ineffective communication, which is often caused by the inequality of roles between parent and child. The role of parental superiority is demonstrated by statements that try to control the child's behavior. The word *you* implies a demand and the use of power that tends to incite rebelliousness in children. The reaction to these "you" statements is understandable when we place ourselves in a similar position. If someone has ever tried to tell you that you were wrong by pointing their finger at you and saying,

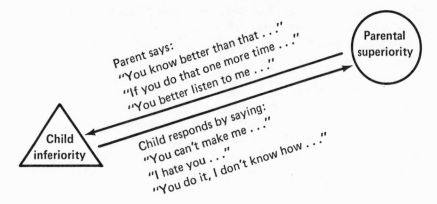

"Aren't *you* the one . . . ?" then you realize why children react in a resentful manner. "You" statements communicate the same message to children and adults. No one likes to be put down. A child is only placed on the defensive when he feels his parents are placing him under attack. "You" statements cause retaliation, rebellion, and discouragement.

Statements made by the parent when disciplining their children should avoid conveying the personal power and superiority of the parent. The power of the social order should rule. "You" statements put the responsibility for changing the child's behavior upon the parents. In a democratic relationship the responsibility for changing one's reactions is self-controlled.

When parents remove themselves from the superior role, they enhance the communication between themselves and their children. The generation gap, which is believed to exist between a large segment of the teen-age population and their parents, is not related to age. It is the inequality of roles between parent and teen-ager that creates a communication gap, not the generation gap. The gap in communication between parents and children can be changed significantly when "I" statements are substituted for ineffective "you" statements.

The parents do not assume the responsibility for change in the child's behavior; there is no demanding. The parents are simply communicating by "I" statements how they respond to the child's misbehavior. These "I" statements allow parents to assume the role of giving guidance to their child on an equal level. The dignity of the child is respected. "I" statements

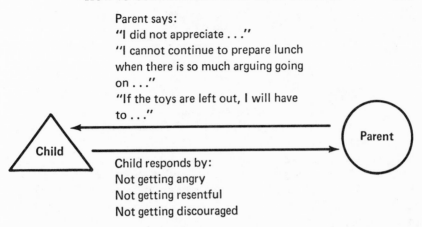

Parent says:
"I did not appreciate . . ."
"I cannot continue to prepare lunch when there is so much arguing going on . . ."
"If the toys are left out, I will have to . . ."

Child

Parent

Child responds by:
Not getting angry
Not getting resentful
Not getting discouraged

do not verbally point an accusing finger at the child, alleviating any possible need for her to become defensive and retaliate against her parents. Although the child may get mad because she is not getting what she wants, "I" statements do not hurt the parent-child relationship because the child's anger is directed at the situation, not the parent.

The situation between Lisa and her father could have been more beneficial to their relationship if the father had used "I" statements.

(Lisa, with head bowed, asks dad to look at and sign the report card.)

MR. ADAMS: I would be glad to look at the report card.

LISA: But I didn't do real good!

MR. ADAMS: Well, it looks like you really put a lot of effort into your art class (encouraging statement).

LISA (with deep feeling): I put a lot of effort into my other subjects also.

MR. ADAMS: Is there anything I can do to help out?

(Lisa is silent, with eyes brimming.)

MR. ADAMS: I can see that this situation is upsetting. Maybe there is something that can be done about it (parent reflects child's feeling).

LISA: Well, I guess I could have studied more (nondefensive response— allows for problem solving to take place).

MR. ADAMS: I think that sounds like a good way to start working on the problem. I'd be glad to help in any way (encouraging statement).

The increase of "I" responses and the decrease of "you" statements (critical statements) by Mr. Adams aptly illustrates four positive outcomes that affect the parent-child relationship. Even though the situation may have negative connotations (bad grade), "I" statements assist in making it a positive learning experience for the child while effectively handling the problem of bad grades. "I" statements maintain open lines of communication, allowing for a healthy relationship; lessen defensive behavior; encourage the building of the child's positive self-concept; and promotes the child's problem-solving and independent living skills.

Two of the major goals of parenting are to help our children develop independent living skills and to help them develop responsible behavior. The use of "I" statements helps achieve these goals. When we eliminate critical "you" statements, our children are allowed to develop the courage to overcome their limitations and to tackle life's tasks.

NONVERBAL COMMUNICATION

The second major area of parent communication deals with the nonverbal messages communicated to children. One of the most easily recognizable nonverbals is the tone of voice used by parents. The effectiveness of "I" statements can be diminished tremendously by using an angry tone of voice. Even the words *I love you* can have a negative meaning, depending on the tone of voice used.

There are other forms of nonverbal communication. When a child never looks at the parent who is talking to him, but goes about his business, he is communicating disinterest. This usually angers parents, yet they do the same thing to their child.

Nonverbal communication takes on added importance when we consider the varied dysfunctions that adversely affect our children's ability to receive and transmit messages. Such nonverbal factors as touch, the distance between the parent and child, eye contact, facial expression, and tone of voice are important to effective communication between parent and child. These nonverbal components may be more important than the actual words parents use to communicate with exceptional children. For "I" statements to have impact on children, parents need to make sure that their verbal and nonverbal messages are the same. This will accurately convey the message parents want their children to receive.

COMMUNICATION COMPONENTS

The inconsistency between what the parent says and what she does (see chapter 12) has the same result of adding confusion to the child's sense of order as does the inconsistency between parent's verbal and nonverbal messages. If they are not the same, children become confused. This confusion has an overall adverse effect upon any disciplinary methods attempted by parents. The following chart presents the various communication components that either significantly enhance or significantly detract from effective communication.

DEVELOPING EFFECTIVE LISTENING SKILLS

Recently a newly trained kindergarten teacher asked advice from the school counselor about a child in her class. She was concerned because Tony only used black paint. Since this appeared to be morbid and peculiar, the counselor said she would talk to Tony and find out if there was anything bothering him that would explain the use of black paint. After talking with Tony, the counselor reported that she could not understand it. The teacher and the counselor agreed to call in the school psychologist to evaluate Tony. The school psychologist saw Tony the next week and administered an extensive battery of tests to try to understand the perplexing situation. The school psychologist reported that he had found no answer to the problem. It was decided at this point that the consulting child psychiatrist be called in because of the difficulty of this case. After a number of sessions with Tony, the psychiatrist gathered no additional information that was helpful in understanding the situation. The growing concern for Tony's use of black paint resulted in a major staff meeting to discuss the issue. During the course of the meeting many hypotheses were discussed. The principal then asked if anybody had ever directly asked Tony why he used only black paint. Everyone silently looked around the room. To the surprise of all the staff it was found that no one had ever asked him! Tony was brought into the room and placed at the head of the table. The principal turned to Tony and said they were all very curious as to why he only used black paint to paint picutures. Timidly Tony looked at the principal and said, "Well, you know Billy Edwards is in my class and he's very, very shy. He's so shy that he's afraid to ask the teacher if he can go to the bathroom. Since he won't ask, he uses the paint jars, and black is the only one he hasn't used yet."

COMMUNICATION

Component	Positive	Negative
Touch	Hold hands	Spank
	Gently place hands on shoulder	Slap
	Embrace—hug	Do not touch at all—lack of physical contact
Distance between parent and child	Sit next to	Stand far apart
	Lean over or bend down	Be in separate rooms
	Stand close to	Talk through window
	No physical barriers between parent and child	Physical barriers between parent and child
Eye contact	Look directly at child	Talk while watching TV
		Talk while reading newspaper
		Talk while doing other work
		No direct eye contact—look the other way
Facial expression	Smile	Look angry, irritated
	Look relaxed	Frown
		Express tension
		Raise eyebrows
		Look cold, icy
Tone of voice	Use moderate level	Yell
	Use pleasant tone	Shout
		Act angry—forceful
Verbal statements	Use "I" statements, such as:	Use "You" statements, such as:
	"I would appreciate . . ."	"You shouldn't do that."
	"I really feel good when . . ."	"You're going to get it."
	"I know it's hard, but . . ."	"Who do you think you are?"

Although this story is humorous, it exemplifies a common difficulty parents have in communicating and understanding their children. The difficulty is that parents make assumptions or jump to conclusions without knowing all the details. One of the ways to understand our children is to develop better listening skills. Parents place themselves in a superior position when they make assumptions that they understand their children without listening to them. Parents and children communicate verbal and nonverbal messages in the exact same way. Once parents become aware of their own communication skills, it becomes easier for them to listen and to understand what their children are communicating. For parents of exceptional children, listening involves not only their ears, but their eyes as well. Effective listening involves both verbal and nonverbal awareness.

The parents who observe that their child comes home from school and becomes disruptive, destructive, and generally irritable easily recognizes that she is communicating through nonverbal behavior that something is bothering her. The spouse who comes home moody and irritable and doesn't like what's for dinner is also communicating an obvious message. The message can be interpreted by observing nonverbal behavior and listening to the message.

Children in general have trouble expressing themselves, but exceptional children may experience more than the usual difficulty. Because of the possible effects their limitations have upon communication with others, exceptional children may rely more heavily on nonverbal behavior such as moodiness, withdrawal, lack of appetite, disruptiveness, and tears. Since these nonverbal signs may be the only way these children have of communicating, parents need to observe changes or variations in their usual ways of acting. These nonverbals are a means of communicating and require the parents' ability and sensitivity to interpret them.

The same skills that parents utilize to understand their children's nonverbal communication should be utilized to understand their children's verbal communication. To communicate effectively we need to make sure we understand what the child's words are really saying. Parents can develop effective listening skills for verbal communication if they recognize and utilize probing and acknowledging statements. If you ask someone, "How are you feeling?" a typical response is, "Oh, all right." It is easy to assume that everything is very good, but for you really to know how the other is, you can use a *probing statement*. "What do you mean, all right?" is one example of a probing statement. "Tell me more" and "I didn't understand what you said" are the types of statements that attempt to draw out more information. With probing statements we can try to find the true meaning behind our children's ambiguous remarks. This information-gathering procedure allows for better listening and understanding of verbal communication with your children. It is also a means of demonstrating the parents' concern for what the child is saying.

When a mother noticed her child having difficulty staying within the lines in the coloring book, she stated, "I know it's upsetting when we try very hard to do something and it doesn't work." This parental response demonstrates an *acknowledging statement*. Acknowledging statements communicate to our children that we understand what they are experiencing. Such statements as "I know you're disappointed," "I see you're scared," "I see that you're upset," and "It looks like you're really enjoying that" convey feeling to the child. Acknowledging statements represent the parents' empathetic understanding of the child's feelings. It also encourages the child to talk about these feelings and not keep them inside. This may avoid future "boilovers" by not allowing negative feelings to build up in the child. One of the characteristics of exceptional children is that they are not very verbal and, therefore, are more inclined to keep their feelings to themselves. When we use probing and acknowledging statements, we help our children to become more conscious of their feelings and to deal more effectively with them.

COMMUNICATION AND MISTAKEN GOALS

Throughout this book the great need for understanding has been emphasized. Purposeful behavior and mistaken goals are demonstrated by all our children to some degree. The following diagrams illustrate how both verbal and nonverbal messages used by parents and children are indicative of certain types of mistaken goals. These diagrams show both effective and ineffective interactions between parents and children. The first two interactions depict communications that perpetuate the mistaken goal of children. The third interaction depicts communication that attempts to diminish the mistaken goal exhibited. The positioning of the child or parent in the diagram represents superior, inferior, or equal communications in the transaction between the parent and child.

The concept of effective communication is the umbrella under which all basic democratic principles fall. Child-rearing principles of encouragement, logical and natural consequences, consistency, and an awareness of the mistaken goals of children's misbehavior are all directed toward developing a

Communication Diagram:
Mistaken Goal I—Undue Attention

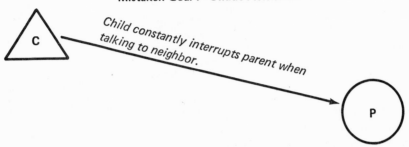

Child's message to parent is: "I need undue attention to feel worthwhile."

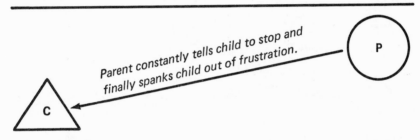

Parent's message to child is: "The more you are able to irritate and frustrate me, the more you will get my attention." (Parental response feeds into child's mistaken goal.)

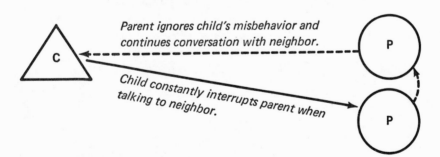

Parent's message to child is: "I will not give you my attention when you misbehave." (Parental response does not feed into child's mistaken goal.)

Communication Diagram: Mistaken Goal II—Power

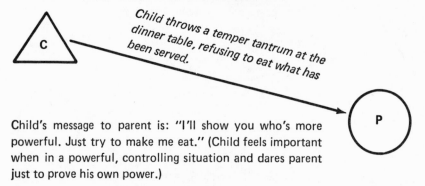

Child's message to parent is: "I'll show you who's more powerful. Just try to make me eat." (Child feels important when in a powerful, controlling situation and dares parent just to prove his own power.)

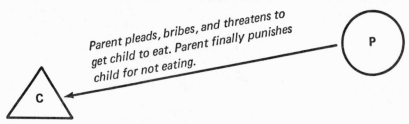

Parent's message to child is: "The more angry you get me, and the more you defy my demands, the more I will use my authority to overpower you and show you who's boss." (Parental response feeds into child's mistaken goal.)

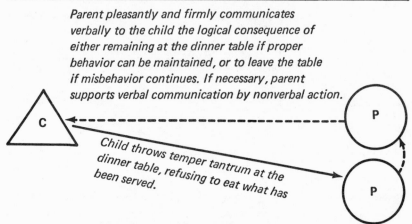

Parent's message to child is: "I will not fall into the trap of trying to over-power you by use of parental authority. I will allow you to choose your own course of behavior and consequence." (Parental response does not feed into child's mistaken goal.)

Communication Diagram: Mistaken Goal III—Revenge

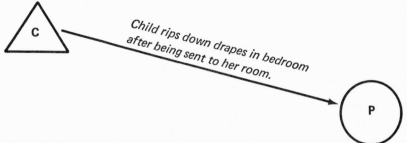

Child's message to parent is: "Since you hurt me, I'll get back at you by destroying something you worked hard at making."

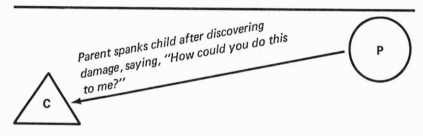

Parent's message to child is: "When you hurt me, I'll hurt you right back." (Parental response feeds into child's mistaken goal.)

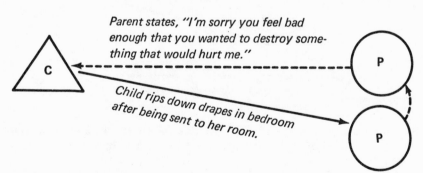

Parent's message to child is: "I acknowledge that you are able to hurt me and recognize that you must be feeling very bad." (Parental response does not feed into mistaken goal. This response may diffuse emotion and open lines of communication.)

Communication Diagram: Mistaken Goal IV—Inadequacy

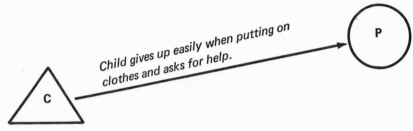

Child's message to parent is: "I'm incapable of doing it. I need you to do it for me."

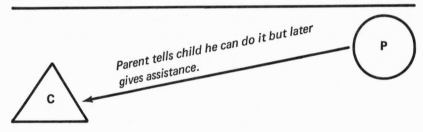

Parent's message to child is: "You are right, you do need my help. You are helpless and incapable." (Parental response feeds into child's mistaken goal.)

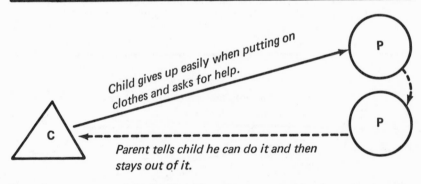

Parent's message to child is: "I believe you are capable of putting on your clothes by yourself." (Parental response does not feed into mistaken goal.)

128

mutually respectful relationship. These principles have been shown to be effective in dealing with children's misbehavior, in building responsible behavior, and in enhancing the relationship between parents and children. The degree to which these principles are effective relies upon both the parents' ability to understand their children's communication and their ability to communicate these principles accurately. If parents wish to have effective lines of communication with all their children, especially their exceptional children, they need to be aware of their own and their children's verbal and nonverbal messages. If parents communicate on equal lines with their children, disciplinary actions can be carried out in a democratic procedure. The parents can thereby communicate that they may not like the behavior, but they still love their children.

Family Atmosphere

21

INCLUDE THE OTHER CHILDREN

Mrs. Lopez is the mother of three children, one of whom is developmentally disabled. A few years ago she read the book *Children: The Challenge,* which outlines democratic child-rearing principles. She learned that fighting among children is often a misdirected way of seeking parental attention. Mrs. Lopez, like many other parents, had fallen into the trap of trying to solve many of her children's hassles. When she realized this, she began to withdraw from her children's fights and told them they would have to work them out themselves. The fighting began to diminish among the children—with one exception. Mrs. Lopez consistently withdrew from the fights except when fights erupted between the other children and Sam, her handicapped child. She would yell at the other children for fighting with him, and she would always come to Sam's rescue. Sam was always getting into fights over toys and never failed to wind up in a fight at the dinner table.

Mrs. Lopez could not understand why the other children so often irritated Sam, promoting chaos around the house. The principle of withdrawal that she used with the other children's fights is based upon the belief that all the children involved in the fights are equally responsible. When she tried to solve the problem and find out who did what to whom, she took away any responsibility for the children to solve the problem and put it all on herself. Mrs.

Lopez found out, as most parents do, that it is virtually impossible to find out who was at fault. By allowing the children to assume equal responsibility for the situation, the parent allows for a *group effect* and feeling of *equality*.

But Mrs. Lopez tried to protect Sam when he got into fights. Treating Sam differently from the other children violated the principle of equality. She did not give Sam the responsibility of solving his own difficulty. Although she consciously wanted everyone to treat Sam as an equal member of the family, her interference demonstrated that he was special. Rather than creating the feeling of a family unit, Mrs. Lopez's inconsistency in dealing with Sam created more competition among the children for special recognition.

If parents of exceptional children want to create a sense of family unity and build equality among the family members, then the principles used need to be applied to all children equally. Rules that apply to some but not others create feelings of unfairness and inequality and spark the development of useless behavior in our children. If children are required to hang up their clothes when they come home, yet they see their father throw his clothes down, they will not feel they are equal. To prevent rebelliousness among our children as well as to develop unity in families with an exceptional child, the practice of equality cannot be segregated among the children or between the parents and children. As long as parents overprotect and make special considerations for their exceptional child, they destroy any possible chance for family unity and enhance the possibility of feelings of inferiority and discouragement in the exceptional child.

Mealtime at the Lopez home as a rule was not pleasant. Sam often exhibited inappropriate behavior while eating, and the other children laughed, encouraging Sam to continue his misbehavior. Mrs. Lopez would attempt to stop Sam's misbehavior, and would yell at the other children to stop laughing. Finally, in an attempt to create more equality and responsibility among the children for their actions, Mrs. Lopez informed all the children before mealtime that any misbehavior was not acceptable at the dinner table—whenever this misbehavior occurred, she would ask them all to leave the dinner table until they could come back and act in a more acceptable way.

Since the children were treated as a group for the misbehavior at mealtime, they became responsible for themselves as well as for the actions of their siblings. Even though Sam may have been the one who initially exhibited inappropriate behavior, the other children's inappropriate response had an important part in the continuance of the misbehavior. The other children reinforced Sam's negative behavior to find their place in the family through positive parental involvement. By encouraging Sam's misbehavior, the other children appeared to be "good" children. The "good" kids attempt to look better than the one who is misbehaving, who is usually the exceptional child. This then places the exceptional child in the position of being the "bad" kid, who finds his place in a useless way through negative behavior. Understanding how each child creates and maintains a specific position in the family shows the importance for dealing with the children as a whole. Taking group action tends to diffuse this type of competition significantly and promotes stronger family unity. In a majority of the conflicts among children it is not just one child misbehaving, for it takes at least two to have a conflict. If parents single one child out, they fulfill their children's mistaken view of a "good" or "bad" kid.

It is not just the parents' responsibility to monitor disruptive behavior. The child who saw his brother going through his father's income tax papers (chapter 6) had a responsibility to do something about it. This sense of social responsibility is developed when parents diminish competition among their children and begin to treat them as equals. If we see someone attempting to break into our neighbor's house, we have a social responsibility to take appropriate action and inform the authorities. This social consciousness is developed by treating children as equals and following them to accept the responsibility for their actions.

22

HAVE FUN AS A FAMILY

In chapter 6 the Levenson family was discussed. Their primary complaint was the inability of the children to play and have fun together. It was common practice for the parents to play with only one child at a time. For example, Johnny would only play such games as checkers with his father. The other children also competed for the parents' individual attention. Although games were being played, there was not a fun, relaxed atmosphere. This concerned the parents. The children didn't appear to enjoy one another. The parents put so much effort into having fun with each child that they actually became exhausted—burnt out—trying to develop a real family atmosphere.

The Levenson family had the right idea in trying to develop a sense of family unity through fun time. However, family unity is not developed by individual family members spending time together, but rather, by the participation of all members. Many parents of exceptional children spend large amounts of time with that child providing special assistance. Although it is necessary, the special help may indirectly create an atmosphere of competition for individual attention, as it did in the Levenson family. This competitive atmosphere does not allow the family members to work together and enjoy one another or develop family unity.

Having fun together is one of the most positive ways of developing cohesiveness among family members. It is through play that all family members relate on an equal basis. The ability to cooperate and share equally are the basic ingredients upon which games and fun time rest. Parents are often the ones who make the rules or take the leadership role. This promotes unequal relationships. But this does not happen when the family plays games—all family members participating in fun time are regulated by a set of rules not established by the parents. This creates an equal opportunity for every family member to participate on an equal level.

The positive practice of fun time among families is traditional but has diminished significantly in today's family. The contemporary family atmosphere cannot be described as one of fun and cooperation between parents and children. It is more aptly described as a continuous battleground. It usually does not revolve around democratic principles but rather focuses upon meeting individual needs. Although contemporary society's attitude is for parents to work hard to provide extensive material benefits for their children, this "doing for" needs to be counterbalanced by "doing with." It is during family fun time that both parents and children can *join* together and construct a feeling of *family*.

Another contemporary trend of our society is the use of television as a nonparticipating form of family entertainment. Family fun time involves equal participation and inter*action* of all family members. Television can be a part of family fun time if we build cooperative and participating activities around it. Television is a passive way of spending time together and does not necessitate any interaction. With television or any other "fun" activity we need to evaluate whether the amount of time spent in that activity ensures a sense of family unity and cooperativeness.

Many parents of exceptional children fail to realize the importance of family fun time and develop a more sober and serious family atmosphere. The mistaken notion of parents that their exceptional child can neither participate in nor benefit from family fun-time activities robs *all* family members of a positive, cooperative experience. The parents' lack of emphasis on family fun time may promote the following unconstructive dynamics in the family:

1. The exclusion of the exceptional child will reinforce her feeling of being different by not being a *regular* part of the family.

2. The exclusion of the exceptional child reinforces the other children's belief that she is different and therefore unequal.

Family fun time is important for all families but holds added significance for families with exceptional children. Because of this importance to exceptional children, certain considerations need to be taken into account in order for the family to maximize the possible benefits from fun time. A major

consideration in choosing family fun-time activities with an exceptional child is that parents need to coordinate the child's limitations with the activity.

The Taft family never had a family fun time at home. They assumed that since their oldest daughter had such limited intellectual ability, she could not adequately participate in organized family activities. One evening during the Christmas holidays they were pleasantly surprised to discover what their daughter was doing while the rest of the family was making Christmas decorations. She observed the other children making simple ornaments and began to imitate them. Everyone's reaction was so surprisingly positive that she beamed from ear to ear. It became obvious from her reaction that she really felt a part of the family's activity. The Taft family learned that all children can enjoy and participate in family activities regardless of their limitations.

For the exceptional child to benefit from these fun family experiences, the parents need to evaluate their child's limitations and adjust the type of activity to those limitations. Another consideration is how to facilitate the exceptional child's maximum participation in the fun activity. Parents have to analyze the child's skills to evaluate what added training might be necessary to help facilitate better adjustment to the play activity. This would limit the potential frustration inherent in activities where the child is deficient in necessary skills. A third consideration in organizing play activities involves the parents' knowledge of the child's ability to adjust to new situations. This is an important consideration because exceptional children rely heavily upon a standard daily routine. Since some fun activities may entail going to new places, they technically involve the breaking of routine and may in fact offer anxiety and stress rather than fun. As shown in chapter 11, Melvin could have been helped to adjust to the sound of the loud whistle on the boat ride. This adjustment, attained by spending a little extra time to prepare Melvin for what was to happen would have increased his enjoyment and participation in the activity.

A final consideration involves the encouragement of even minimal participation in the fun activity. All family fun experiences do not permit equal participation of all the children. The parents' responsibility is to encourage participation, even though it may not be equal, to develop the cohesive feeling generated by family activities. This is most evident in spectator activities. Some family members may be actively participating while others watch. Although cheering for their brothers or sisters may be the total amount of involvement, their participation should still be actively encouraged. It is not how much they are involved, it is *being involved.*

The following rules are suggested to help alleviate difficulties and facilitate the establishment of family fun time in familes with exceptional children.

1. Utilize the family council to set up and plan family fun activities (see chapter 23).
2. Establish a daily time for family activity.
3. Be concerned about the quality, not the quantity, of time. Establish activity time to child's attention span. At first, activities may be of a short duration.
4. Help choose activities that are not beyond the exceptional child's ability level.
5. Suggestions for family activities should come from all family members.
6. Initial participation from children may be slight, but continued parental enthusiasm is contagious. Be consistent.
7. If activity invokes winning or losing, parental emphasis should be placed on the enjoyment of spending time together, to diminish possible competitiveness.
8. Do not select activities that would eliminate a family member.

The Hess family liked playing games as a group. One game that could have been very enjoyable ended up in frustration and tension because it entailed the throwing of dice, which Rose, who had cerebral palsy, had great difficulty with. She wanted to participate yet did not want others to throw the dice for her. But in her attempts the dice usually ended up all over the room. This disrupted the flow of the game and irritated the other children.

At a family council meeting (see chapter 23), the Hess family brought up the problem of Rose's participation in the game. They decided to use a dice turner from an old game they had. All the family members agreed to use the dice turner to eliminate any special treatment of Rose. By doing this the family was again able to enjoy family fun time. Although the modification was simple, it was aimed at Rose's particular dysfunction, and encouraged her equal participation in the activity.

The old-fashioned idea of the family being fun has lost its meaning in today's society. This type of fun atmosphere needs to be rekindled in our homes. It is through activities such as family fun time that family unity and cohesiveness are built. Family members who are able to enjoy each other's company develop a feeling of harmony that can last for a lifetime. It is this harmony that creates a pleasant and cooperative family atmosphere.

23

THE WEEKLY FAMILY
COUNCIL MEETING

The family council is the vehicle by which all democratic principles can be initiated in families with exceptional children. The family council is in itself democracy at work. As the name implies, it is a weekly family meeting during which all family members plan fun activities and solve family concerns. The family council operates through the use of democratic principles, which lead to the development of harmonious family living. It also uses the problem-solving ability inherent in groups to solve family difficulties cooperatively.

THE CONSENSUS RULE

A family council was being conducted at the Stephens home to decide where the family was to go on this year's vacation. After a lengthy discussion on the various possibilities the three children wanted to take a twelve-hundred-mile trip to Disney World. The parents wanted to rent a cabin at a nearby state park. If a vote were taken and a decision were based upon majority rule, disharmony would be created between the parents and children. Disney World could not be a realistic choice because of the financial burden and the time restraints placed upon the family. Because the parents were unable to adhere to the majority decision, the children felt betrayed and angry.

In a *true* democratic family structure each family member's opinion has equal weight in the decision-making process. Since the Stephens family used majority rule, those who fell in the minority (going to the state park) were not taken into consideration on the final selection. In the use of majority rule a win-lose situation is always created, rather than a cohesive-cooperative problem-solving body. A true democratic problem-solving body mandates the use of consensus rather than majority rule, which utilizes the power of numbers rather than individual logic. Reaching a mutually agreed upon decision demonstrates the practice of human equality.

Exceptional children are typically not treated equally. This creates feelings of inferiority, but the principle of consensus and equal representation in the family council may help to offset the inferiority of such feelings.

When a consensus of opinion is not reached, as in the Stephens family, no immediate decision should be made. In mutual problem solving, all parties need to take into consideration the logic and the rationale of the others' opinion. The parents should try to understand that the children want excitement on a vacation. The children need to understand the financial situation and the time restraint affecting the parents' decision. Often a third alternative is developed before a mutually agreed-upon decision occurs. If the group does not come up with a consensus, no action is taken.

NEED FOR CONSISTENT ROUTINE

One predominant characteristic relied upon by children of all ages, especially exceptional children, is a consistent family routine. This consistency of routine assures children of their sense of security, since they can know what is expected from them (see chapter 12). In setting up the family council, the parents need to be aware of structuring this activity in a routine manner.

The family council meeting is held weekly; the day and time should remain as consistent as possible, establishing a family routine by which the children's sense of order is maintained. Exceptional children may have greater difficulty in adapting to changes in routine, therefore mandating the need for a routine family council. Consistency is also required by the many outside activities that tend to disrupt family structure. Without this consistency it would be almost impossible to coordinate the family council with all the outside activities in which each family member participates. By doing this the family council becomes the focal part of that day and the outside activities revolve around the family council.

Practicing democratic principles begins when the time for the family council is being selected, usually at the first meeting of the council. The cooperative behavior that parents are trying to teach their children can be modeled by developing a consensus as to the best possible day and time for the meeting. A discussion should be held to evaluate each family member's outside activities that may interfere with the suggested day and time. This process lays the foundation for future meetings, when the use of consensus of opinion will be the avenue to democratic family decision making.

The Stephens family came to a consensus to hold their family council meetings on Sunday evenings because outside activities were few and all family members were usually home preparing for the start of a new week. At the initial meeting, when the Stephens family established their family council routine, the parents assumed the major responsibility in demonstrating the democratic principles involved in reaching a consensus of opinion. This was done because of the children's lack of experience and knowledge in democratic procedures.

THE EQUALITY OF THE EXCEPTIONAL CHILD

At a meeting of a study group for parents of exceptional children the Davis family asked how a family council could benefit their family, since their daughter Tracey has limited speech and intellectual ability. They felt that a family council that promotes family equality would be useless to Tracey, who is unable to participate on an equal level. The group attempted to get the Davises to understand that if Tracey is participating to the best of her ability, she is participating as an equal family member, although she is functioning at a different level. Even in difficult cases, as in the Davis family, the child's mere presence at the family council is enough to create the sense of family unity and cohesiveness, which is one of the major purposes of a family council.

In families with children who are severely limited in their ability to participate at the same level of the other children, there are two predominant advantages for establishing a family council. The first advantage is that the exceptional child is allowed to *feel* a part of the group and tends to avoid the discouraging feeling of being left out. If the exceptional child is excluded, his potential for developing the feeling of not being OK may increase significantly. Excluding a young child may have the same effect. The earlier children get involved, even by sitting on mom's or dad's lap, the more they will feel a part of the group. When children are excluded because of age or physical and intellectual limitations, they will usually feel different and not a part of the group.

The second major advantage relates to the other children in the family. The family council provides children a sense of belonging by providing a forum to share their ideas and feelings. Because of the amount of special assistance usually given to the exceptional child, the family council provides a vehicle for the other children to receive constructive recognition and time from their parents. Parents often erroneously assume that the other children are able to solve almost all their problems on their own. This is offset by the family council, which demonstrates to the other children that their parents are concerned with them as well as with their exceptional sibling. In families with an exceptional child, the other children often look upon the exceptional child as set apart. When everyone functions together in the family council, the others begin to see the exceptional child as being a part of the family. This togetherness helps to diminish any emphasis that might have been placed upon individual differences. This enhances the feelings in the other children of belonging to a "true" family, rather than a family "with" an exceptional child.

GROUND RULES

To establish a family council and to have it operate as successfully as possible, the following ground rules must be followed:

1. All decisions in the family council should be made from a consensus of agreement, not a majority vote. This will help ensure equal participation of all members. Parents, because of common parental roles, may have to monitor their participation so as not to control the decision-making process. To avoid parental control and to demonstrate equality, the chairperson is different for each meeting.

2. A mutually agreed-upon day and time for the weekly family council should be established as soon as possible and adhered to as consistently as possible. The meetings may initially be short, increasing in length as needs dictate. The duration must take into account the exceptional child's attention span.

3. The attendance of all family members should be encouraged but is not required to hold the family council meeting. If a family member is

unable to attend a meeting or chooses not to participate at a meeting, the family council should still be held. All family members should be aware that if someone chooses not to attend a meeting, he is still responsible for whatever group decisions are made.

4. Any decisions that are agreed upon at a family council meeting are to be upheld until they can be reconsidered at the following weekly family council meeting. If someone in the family realizes in the middle of the week that the decision she agreed to is not exactly what was expected, she is still responsible for carrying out the agreement until it can be discussed at the next meeting.

5. Emergency family council meetings are not a common occurrence. However, an emergency meeting can be held if all family members agree that the situation is serious enough to warrant an emergency meeting.

6. Canceling a family council meeting is not recommended, and should be avoided if at all possible. As with calling an emergency family council meeting, a unanimous agreement is needed to cancel the regularly scheduled meeting. Calling emergency meetings and canceling regularly scheduled meetings would change the standard family routine and may adversely affect the exceptional child's behavior.

7. Topics or issues that cannot be decided upon by a family consensus should not be presented to the family for a decision. If the family needs to move because the parent who is in the military is being transferred out of state, the decision does not lie with the family. Rather, the topic could focus upon feelings about moving and things family members feel need to be taken into consideration about the move.

8. The focus of the family council meetings should be on a variety of common family concerns and planning fun activities. Although problems in the family are discussed, it should not turn into a gripe session but rather remain a problem-solving session. Family members will not want to participate in a family council if only negative criticisms and complaints are given. The emphasis on the positive should be maintained.

9. The flexibility on the part of all family members in the family council with exceptional children is absolutely mandatory for success. It is necessary to adapt democratic principles around the exceptional child to maximize their potential involvement. This can be seen when the family discusses such things as responsibilities around the house. Although it's true that these decisions are usually made on a week-by-week basis,

exceptional children may require a longer period of time for assuming a specific responsibility in order to develop skills in that area. Consistently changing chores would not allow for skill development to occur. It is the flexibility within the structure of the family council that allows the exceptional child to participate as an equal member of the family.

The family council provides parents the opportunity to share responsibility with their children. The ability to assume responsibility as early as possible builds a sense of independence as well as cohesiveness within the family. Since parents cannot tell their children how to solve problems, the family council is a vehicle by which the problem-solving process is practiced under parental guidance. The family council should become an integral part of every home because all the democratic principles that have been presented are incorporated in its operation.

24

ENJOY YOUR CHILDREN

The realization that perfect parenting is impossible sometimes comes as a shock to many parents. However, an even greater shock is experienced when parents learn that it is not only OK to make mistakes, but that it is also normal. One of the pitfalls parents are faced with is their feeling of having to deal with every misbehavior successfully. Parents need to learn to relax and accept their inevitable imperfections as human beings. The misbehaviors of children present a difficult challenge to parents. Exceptional children are an even greater challenge to today's child-rearing skills. Parents of exceptional children need to realize that it is impossible always to know the *best* course of action, the best solution to a misbehavior. One of the reasons it is impossible is because many of the situations are so complex and may be virtually impossible to correct. The first step to becoming truly good parents is to realize that parents cannot do everything for their children. They can't solve every problem presented. Parenting is not an easy job, but learning how to relax as a parent and not to jump at every annoyance is a major characteristic of effective parenting.

Mary is the mother of four young children. At dinner time Mary never seems to have time for herself and never eats an entire hot meal. Because of the muscle coordination problem of her oldest daughter, Mary cuts her daughter's food into small portions so it is manageable. The other children used to demand that she cut up their food also. This continued for a long time because of Mary's need to give the same amount of attention to all her children. It was not until she attended a study group for parents of exceptional children that she began to look at her family objectively and understand the family structure with the exceptional child. Mary began to focus upon the competition among the children and how her reaction unintentionally reinforced this useless behavior. Mary realized the purpose of her children's behavior and how her need to be fair and give equal treatment reinforced their mistaken goals. She then knew that her overconcern to be fair and create an harmonious family atmosphere really fostered the competition among the children. The more concerned Mary was with trying to be fair and do everything for everybody, the more the children used it against her to fulfill their own goals.

Mary is like many other parents of exceptional children. Before parents can be more relaxed in the family, they must realize that they do not need to and cannot solve every problem that arises.

"What did I do to deserve this?" is the common reaction of a frustrated parent of an exceptional child. This frustration pushes many parents to develop the belief that to be a responsible parent they have to give up their own life for the exceptional child. Putting their own personal needs aside actually diminishes their effectiveness as parents. If parents deny their own needs, they wind up doing for their children out of a feeling of *having to* rather than *wanting to*. Parents who are able to acknowledge that they have personal needs and try to meet them will allow their children to develop on their own. This fosters independence. Parents can still put the same amount of energy toward guiding their children, but the energy will be toward fostering independent behavior rather than creating and maintaining dependent behaviors.

When parents are able to acknowledge their own needs, they develop a more optimistic, encouraging attitude toward all their children, and they become aware of the goals of misbehavior and understand family dynamics. These characteristics enhance the opportunity for children to develop independence and responsibility, and to enjoy life more. The more capable our children become in handling life's tasks, the greater the enjoyment and parental satisfaction. By understanding our children and implementing democratic child-rearing practices of family living, we may all come to share the feeling expressed by one mother when she said, "I used to love my children, but now that I'm able to relax, I also like them.

Appendixes

APPENDIX 1

LEARNING ACTIVITIES WORKBOOK

We feel that the philosophy presented in this book subscribes to the fullest meaning of "human equality." Equality is crucial in the development of close relationships and family unity. Our purpose in providing this appendix was first, to stimulate your involvement in your readings; second, to help give you a clearer understanding of the child-rearing philosophy presented in this book; third, to provide you with an individualized working guide for the application of the principles presented; and last, to help foster your active participation in the process of constructive guidance for your children.

This appendix is structured into eight sessions for your individual learning, giving you a step-by-step, systematic approach for applying the principles found in this book to your family. Clearly organized assignments and learning activities with charts are presented to aid you in your efforts toward building family unity. Most of the sessions contain two parts. Part 1 states the chapters to be read and presents a self-examination, while part 2 provides you with an activity to implement the basic principles you have read.

The material presented in this appendix has been adapted from: *A Parents' Guide to Children: The Challenge* (New York: Hawthorn Books, 1978).

SESSION 1—SETTING YOUR GOALS

Part 1

Take some time to think about your family. You may want to consider some of the following ideas:

1. How do you and your children interact?

2. How do you interact with your exceptional child?

3. How does the rest of the family react to the exceptional child?

4. How much time do the members of your family spend with one another? Does this time involve arguing, fun time, mealtime, problem solving, special training?

5. How much time do you spend correcting your children's misbehavior?

Part 2

Now that you have taken time out to think about your family's interaction, follow through by formulating some goals. Using the sheet printed here, record what you would like to achieve for both your family and yourself. See the sample goals chart #1 and then fill out your objectives.

Explanation of Goal-Setting Chart #1

The following chart is one of the most important aids in finding the solu- tions to difficulties you are now experiencing with your children.

To accomplish this task, you must set goals that are specific and obtainable. This requires consideration of physical and intellectual limitations of the exceptional child. The procedure for accomplishing this task includes the setting of both child and family goals.

Child Goal: A behavior or attitude exhibited by the exceptional child.

Family Goal: A behavior or attitude exhibited by most of the family.

You will find the sample goals on the next page. Sample #1 is good, but the goals are too broad in scope and unrealistic, not taking into consideration the child's limitations. Sample #2 shows examples of the same basic ideas, but *more specifically stated* and *realistic*.

SETTING GOALS FOR YOUR FAMILY
Chart #1 (Sample)

	Goals	Limitations	Time Element
Sample 1			
Family	1. Have a more harmonious family	None	7 mos.
Exceptional child	1. Develop good speaking vocabulary	Brain damage affecting speech	3 mos.
	2. Develop good etiquette at dinner table	Severe intellectual dysfunction	2 mos.
Sample 2			
Family	1. Less fighting among the children and with parents	None	7 mos.
Exceptional child	1. Develop basic speech sounds	Brain damage affecting speech	1 yr.
	2. Refrain from throwing food on floor	Severe intellectual dysfunction	2 mos.

SETTING GOALS FOR YOUR FAMILY
Chart #1

	Goals	Limitations	Time Element
Family	1.		
	2.		
	3.		
Exceptional Child	1.		
	2.		
	3.		

SESSION 2—BASIC PRINCIPLES IN UNDERSTANDING CHILD DEVELOPMENT

Part 1

1. Readings:

Chapter

1. Child Rearing in Our Contemporary Society
2. Development of Behavior Patterns in Children
3. Characteristics of Exceptional Children
4. Common Behavior Patterns of Exceptional Children
5. Characteristics of the Exceptional Parent
6. The Exceptional Child: The Effects on Other Children

2. Evaluate your learning by doing the self-examination included.

Self-Examination

After you have completed your readings, try this self-examination to help highlight key principles and bring into focus new ideas.

CIRCLE CORRECT ANSWER

1. The authors speak of equality between parents and children as a relationship based upon: (A) Children being able to do whatever adults do. (B) Freedom without responsibility. (C) Parents doing whatever they want to do. (D) Mutual respect.

2. Autocratic methods of child rearing: (A) Are outdated and ineffective. (B) Should be used by parents today. (C) Work well with certain types of children. (D) Work well if applied correctly.

3. Societal attitudes toward the exceptional child are changing as more emphasis is placed on: (A) Democratic principles, or equality. (B) Autocratic principles. (C) Freedom. (D) Parental authority.

4. All children's behaviors are affected by the need to: (A) Get ahead in society. (B) Belong and find a place in the group. (C) Dominate their siblings. (D) Put parents in their control.

5. Purposive behavior is characteristic of: (A) Exceptional children. (B) Fully functioning children. (C) Juvenile delinquents. (D) All children.

6. The impact of a child's handicap is determined by: (A) The type of

handicap. (B) How the handicap was incurred. (C) The limiting factors of the handicap. (D) How the child interprets the handicap.

7. Although all children exhibit misbehavior, exceptional children may sometimes present actions that the parents feel are misbehaviors, but are actually: (A) Characteristics of exceptional children because they tend to misbehave more than other children. (B) The behavioral characteristics of the child's disability. (C) Misbehaviors. (D) None of the above.

8. Exceptional children usually maintain certain negative behaviors because: (A) No one pays attention to the behavior. (B) The exceptional child gets a desirable payoff from the behavior. (C) Exceptional children have absolutely no control over their behaviors. (D) The exceptional child doesn't know any better.

9. In the family constellation what will have the greatest effect on siblings finding their places? (A) The influence of the children upon one another. (B) The influence of the parents. (C) Child-rearing practices. (D) Values and morals.

10. Behavioral characteristics that occur naturally in exceptional children can best be defined as: (A) Behavioral characteristics that are associated with certain dysfunctions. (B) Behavioral characteristics that occur outdoors. (C) Behavioral characteristics that occur indoors. (D) All of the above.

11. Understanding behaviors that occur naturally is important because: (A) They may begin to appear as a misbehavior in and of themselves. (B) They may have the effect of accenting already existing behavior. (C) Both A and B. (D) It is not important.

12. Temper tantrums: (A) Cannot be controlled in exceptional children. (B) Are uncommon in exceptional children. (C) Are a result of the disability. (D) Are an effective means that all children use to control parents' behavior.

13. Which of the following is not a major behavior pattern of the exceptional child? (a) Pamperedness. (B) Discouragement. (C) Stealing. (D) Overcompensation.

14. When there is an exceptional child in the family, it is common for other siblings to respond by being: (A) Competitive with each other. (B) Protective of the exceptional sibling. (C) Imitative of undesirable behaviors of the exceptional sibling. (D) All of the above.

15. In attempting to recognize and prevent negative behavior patterns from developing in siblings of exceptional children, it is most important for parents to remember: (A) Misbehavior by exceptional children cannot

be stopped. (B) Misbehavior by all children cannot be stopped. (C) All behavior is directed toward finding one's place. (D) It is impossible for the siblings to find their place in a positive way.

Part 2

Your learning activity for this phase is to complete charts #1 and #2.

Explanation of Chart #1

Chart #1 is designed to help parents focus on the negative feelings that they may have had or are currently experiencing. The purpose of the chart is to illustrate the feelings the parents have toward themselves and others. The following questions are designed to pinpoint those areas of most concern. In this manner, we can concentrate on the understanding of these feelings and how we can make the necessary changes in how we feel, since these feelings can adversely affect our relationship with the exceptional child.

1. Do you find that this feeling occurs when you interact with those family members concerning the exceptional child? (Yes or No)
2. Do you find this feeling to be a problem? (Yes or No)
3. Does the problem occur: (A) Often. (B) Sometimes. (C) Very little.

The sample illustrates a parent's response pattern of feelings. The results demonstrate that he has guilt feelings in himself, with his spouse, and in his relationship with his exceptional child. He also feels pity toward his exceptional child. The chart also shows that he exhibits a great deal of anger, which is often displayed toward the other children. He also tends to have negative feelings toward his spouse. The particular feelings, to which this parent answered "yes," "yes," and "often" are the feelings that need immediate attention (circled).

Fill out chart #1 by starting with the feeling of being overwhelmed and going across the top of the chart. Ask yourself the three questions concerning this feeling related to yourself, your spouse, and so on. Then proceed to the second feeling (rejection) and continue the same process. When you complete the whole chart, circle the areas that show up to be the most problematic.

PARENTAL FEELING CHART #1 (SAMPLE)

	Self	Spouse	Exceptional Child	Other Sibling(s)	Persons Outside Home	Others
Overwhelmed						
Rejection		1. Yes 2. Yes 3. Sometimes				
Denial						
Anger				1. Yes 2. Yes 3. Often		
Pity			1. Yes 2. Yes 3. Often			
Jealousy					1. Yes 2. Yes 3. Little	
Guilt	1. Yes 2. Yes 3. Often	1. Yes 2. Yes 3. Often	1. Yes 2. Yes 3. Often			
Bitterness						

PARENTAL FEELING CHART #1

	Self	Spouse	Exceptional Child	Other Sibling(s)	Persons Outside Home	
verwhelmed						
ejection						
enial						
nger						
ty						
ealousy						
uilt						
tterness						

This chart will help you become aware of the interaction of the misbehavior and characteristics of the child's handicap.

CHART #2 (SAMPLE)

Child's Misbehavior	Characteristic of Child's Handicap That Influences Misbehavior
1. Constantly picks at fabric pulls	1. Perseveration
2. Refuses to dress self even though capable	2. Poor muscle coordination

CHART #2

Child's Misbehavior	Characteristic of Child's Handicap That Influences Misbehavior
1.	1.
2.	2.
3.	3.
4.	4.

SESSION 3—BASIC PRINCIPLES IN DEALING WITH EXCEPTIONAL CHILDREN

Part 1

1. Readings:

   Chapter

   7. The Purpose of Misbehavior

   8. Encouragement—Building the Positives

   9. Logical Consequences

   10. Natural Consequences

2. Study Child's Mistaken Goals—chart #1, page 161.

3. Evaluate your learning by doing the self-examination included.

Explanation of Child's Mistaken Goals—Chart #1

Chart 1 (Adapted from information presented by Vicki Soltz in her *Study Group Leader's Manual* [Chicago: Alfred Adler Institute, 1967], pp. 71–74) has been included for the purpose of helping each parent understand the goals of all children's misbehavior by understanding the emotional reaction (feeling) in the parent that is typically associated with a child's particular goal.

EXAMPLE

Emotional Reaction	Mistaken Goal
Annoyed, Frustrated	Attention Getting

CHILD'S MISTAKEN GOALS
Chart #1

Consistent Misbehavior	Emotional Reaction (of parent)	Mistaken Goal
he showoff alking question mark akes minor mischief ashfulness istability earfulness nxiety ntidiness	Annoyed Frustrated Wants to remind Coaxing Delighted with "good child"	Attention
"rebel" emper tantrums awdling aziness tubbornness isobedience ad habits ntruthfulness	Mad Upset Provoked Generally wants power Challenged—"I'll *make* him do it." "You can't get away with it."	Power
ealing ed wetting iolent and brutal ullen and defiant vicious" violent passivity"	Hurt "How could she do this to me?"	Revenge
Hopeless"	Despair—hopeless "I give up."	Inadequacy

Self-Examination

After you have completed your readings, try this self-examination to help highlight key principles and bring into focus new ideas.

CIRCLE CORRECT ANSWER

1. The typical feeling a parent has when in a power struggle with his child is: (A) Annoyed, hurt, frustrated. (B) Angry, mad, upset. (C) Hurt, annoyed, hopeless. (D) Frustrated, upset, angry.

2. The belief "Since things are not done the way I want them to be, I will get back at people for not allowing me to do what I want to do" falls into which mistaken goal? (A) Attention. (B) Power. (C) Revenge. (D) Inadequacy.

3. The child who consistently feels there is no hope, feels useless, and expects to meet with failure would be which mistaken goal? (A) Attention. (B) Power. (C) Revenge. (D) Inadequacy.

4. Which of the following is an encouraging statement? (A) You did a nice job cleaning your room. (B) You did a fine job washing the floor, I'm so proud of you. (C) What a good boy you are for eating all your breakfast! (D) What a good girl you are for not spilling any milk!

5. Children with the mistaken goal of power believe: (A) I'm only OK when I get what I want. (B) I'm only OK when everyone pays attention to me. (C) Everything will work out OK. (D) Nothing will work out OK.

6. The use of encouragement mandates that we: (A) Overexaggerate our feelings when our children do well. (B) Never get angry at our children. (C) Separate the doer from the act. (D) Encourage every positive action by our children.

7. A difference between encouragement and praise is: (A) Praise separates the doer from his actions. (B) Praise can be used only when a child fails. (C) Encouragement separates the "doer" from her actions. (D) Encouragement can only be used when a child succeeds.

8. Encouragement ought to be used: (A) Only when the child fails. (B) Only when the child does something very well. (C) Only when praise fails. (D) All the way through the learning process.

9. In a logical consequence: (A) The child has no choice in the outcome of the situation. (B) The child has a choice in the outcome of the situation. (C) The parent has no choice in the outcome of the situation. (D) The consequence occurs with no parental involvement.

10. What is meant by a logical consequence is: (A) There is a direct relation-

ship between the consequence and the child's actions. (B) There is no relationship between the consequence and the child's action. (C) There is a logical relationship between the parents and children. (D) There is no relationship between the parents and children.

11. Caution needs to be taken when using logical consequences with power-oriented children because: (A) It is difficult for power children to be logical. (B) Power children cannot make their own choices. (C) If the parent is angry, the child tends to perceive the parent as being silly. (D) If the parent is angry, the consequence tends to be seen as a punishment by the child.

12. The best definition of a natural consequence is: (A) It demonstrates the presence of reality and its effect, with parental involvement. (B) It demonstrates the presence of reality and its effect, without parental involvement. (C) It demonstrates a consequence of a child's behavior that a parent sets up. (D) It demonstrates a consequence of the child's behavior after a choice has been given by the parent.

13. One reason parents of exceptional children may feel hesitant in using natural consequences is: (A) The consequences are really a form of punishment. (B) The consequences are really a form of permissiveness. (C) They may wish to protect their children from any further discomfort since the child already has to cope with a handicap. (D) Exceptional children can't handle frustrations in life.

14. The distinction between natural consequences and punishment is: (A) Natural consequences express the power of reality and punishment expresses the power of the parent. (B) Natural consequences express the power of the parent and punishment represents the power of reality. (C) Punishment requires less involvement by the parent. (D) There is no distinction.

15. Natural consequences should be avoided when: (A) You don't have time. (B) The child knows what is going to happen. (C) There is the possibility of physical harm coming to the child. (D) Dealing with a power-oriented child.

Part 2

Your learning activity for this phase is to complete charts #1, #2, and #3.

Explanation of Chart #1

To determine your children's mistaken goals, you need to identify how *you felt* when the misbehavior took place. This chart will identify the mistaken goal associated with your feelings, as well as the physiological characteristics of the child's dysfunction that accentuates the mistaken goal.

CHART #1 (SAMPLE)

Your Child's Misbehavior + Your Feelings = Your Child's Mistaken Goal

Consistent Misbehavior	How did you feel?		Goal	Physiological Characteristics
1. Constantly picks at fabric pulls.	Frustrated–annoyed	√	Attention	Perseveration
	Mad–upset		Power	
	Hurt		Revenge	
	Like giving up; it is hopeless		Inadequacy	
1. Refuses to dress self, even though capable.	Frustrated–annoyed		Attention	Poor muscle coordination
	Mad–upset	√	Power	
	Hurt		Revenge	
	Like giving up; it is hopeless		Inadequacy	

CHART #1

Your Child's Misbehavior + Your Feelings = Your Child's Mistaken Goal

Consistent Misbehavior	How did you feel?	Goal	Physiological characteristics
	Frustrated—annoyed	Attention	
	Mad—upset	Power	
	Hurt	Revenge	
	Like giving up; it is hopeless	Inadequacy	
	Frustrated—annoyed	Attention	
	Mad—upset	Power	
	Hurt	Revenge	
	Like giving up; it is hopeless	Inadequacy	

Explanation of Chart #2

By filling out chart #2 you will follow four steps in the development of appropriate remedial procedures for the consistent misbehavior exhibited.

The information you need to place in the first three columns (Consistent Misbehavior, Goal, and Physiological Characteristics) is the same as information you provided in chart #1, p. 165.

CHART #2 (SAMPLE)

Your Child's Misbehavior + Your Feelings = Your Child's Mistaken Goal			Logical or Natural Consequence
Consistent Misbehavior	Goal	Physiological Characteristics	
1. Constantly picks at fabric pulls	√ Attention 　 Power 　 Revenge 　 Inadequacy	Perseveration	Not allowed to wear double-knit fabric for set number of days if misbehavior continues after being informed of consequence (logical).
2. Refuses to dress self, even though capable	Attention √ Power 　 Revenge 　 Inadequacy	Poor muscle coordination	Since child refuses to get dressed by self, child is taken into car as is when time to leave (logical).

CHART #2

Your Child's Misbehavior + Your Feelings = Your Child's Mistaken Goal

Consistent Misbehavior	Goal	Physiological Characteristics	Logical or Natural Consequences
	Attention		
	Power		
	Revenge		
	Inadequacy		
	Attention		
	Power		
	Revenge		
	Inadequacy		

Explanation of Chart #3

Use of chart #3 will allow you to see how much you are encouraging your children and where more encouragement is needed. In using this chart, record your behavior toward all the children, so the full pattern emerges. Remember, you want to be aware of any tendency on your part to treat the child as special.

(Sample—Child A, Exceptional Child)

Day 1—√ Mother found two occasions for encouraging her child for attempting to get dressed.

Day 2—√ Mother found two occasions for encouraging her child for attempting to get dressed.

Day 3—√ Mother found four occasions for encouraging her child for attempting to get dressed.

(Sample—Child B, Other Child in Family)

Day 1—√ Mother found one occasion for encouraging her child for cooperating at the supermarket.

Day 2—√ Mother found two occasions for encouraging her child for attempting to do chores.

Day 3—√ Mother found four occasions for encouraging her child's positive behaviors.

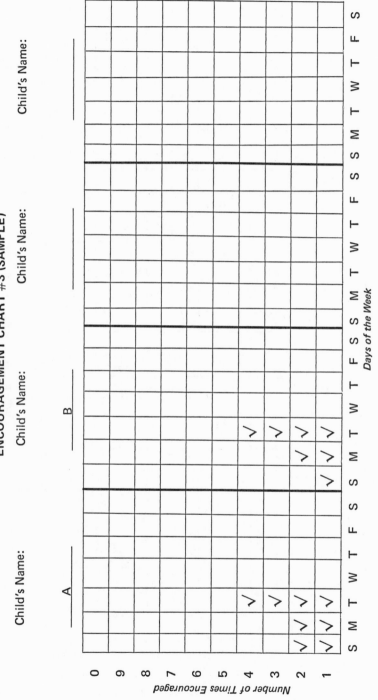

ENCOURAGEMENT CHART #3 (SAMPLE)

Child's Name:

Child's Name:

Child's Name:

Child's Name:

Number of Times Encouraged

Days of the Week

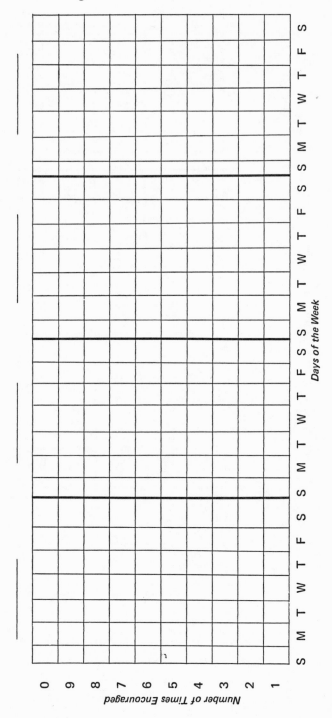

ENCOURAGEMENT CHART #3

Child's Name:

Child's Name:

Child's Name:

Child's Name:

Days of the Week

Number of Times Encouraged

SESSION 4—IMPLEMENTATION OF BASIC PRINCIPLES

Part 1

1. Review encouragement chart.
2. Discuss the implementation of the logical or natural consequences developed in chart #2, session 3.

Part 2

Your learning activity for this phase is to complete chart #1 on the use of logical or natural consequences as a remedial procedure. The process of developing appropriate remedial procedures follows the same outline as in charts #1 and #2, session 3.

CHART #1

Consistent Misbehavior	Logical or Natural Consequence
1.	1.
2.	2.
3.	3.
4.	4.

SESSION 5—FACTORS TO BE MAINTAINED IN RAISING EXCEPTIONAL CHILDREN

Part 1

1. Readings:

    Chapter   11. Avoid Drastic Routine Changes

                  12. Consistency: The Key Factor in Changing Misbehavior

                  13. A Stitch in Time Saves Nine

                  14. Actions Speak Louder Than Words

                  15. The Bathroom Technique: A Lesson in Positive Withdrawal

                  16. Avoid Reinforcing Negative Behavior

2. Study the Mistaken Goals chart, page 174.

3. Evaluate your learning by doing the self-examination included.

Self-Examination

After you have completed your readings, try this self-examination. This will help to highlight key principles and bring into focus new ideas.

CIRCLE CORRECT ANSWER

1. What does a set routine usually do for children? (A) It gives them a reason to misbehave. (B) It gives them a feeling of insecurity. (C) It gives them a sense of disorder. (D) It gives them a feeling of security and sense of order.

2. The more inconsistent and irregular the daily routine the more likely the exceptional child will become: (A) Easily confused. (B) Overexcited. (C) Highly emotional. (D) All of the above.

3. What will typically happen to the child's misbehavior when a parent begins a consistent method of redirection? (A) It will stop immediately. (B) Misbehavior will initially increase. (C) Child will change to a new behavior. (D) It will have no effect at all.

4. Why does it take time for a child's misbehavior to change? (A) Everything takes time. (B) Behaviors are hard to change. (C) Time will positively change all behaviors. (D) It took time for the child to learn the misbehavior.

5. When parents are consistent in dealing with their children, what usually happens is: (A) The child resents this. (B) It confuses the child as to

what is expected of him. (C) The child knows what is expected of him, and it establishes a sense of order. (D) It establishes a sense of disorder.

6. The principle followed by parents to postpone the taking of action is called: (A) Logical consequence. (B) Hope method. (C) Natural consequence. (D) Encouragement.

7. According to the authors, the phrase "A stitch in time saves nine" means: (A) If we act while the problem is small, it will only use up our time and energy in the future. (B) If we act while the problem is small, we will avoid putting time and energy into solving a greater problem in the future. (C) We should wait until the problem becomes bigger. (D) Hope the problem goes away by itself.

8. Logical reasoning that is verbally communicated by parents is often ineffective because: (A) Parents are illogical. (B) Parents act without regard for the child. (C) Children act on their own private logic. (D) children don't listen.

9. Children learn what is expected of them when: (A) The parent tells the child she will be punished if she doesn't obey. (B) The parents reward the child's positive behavior. (C) The parents are lenient. (D) The parents' verbal statements are supported by their actions.

10. In the bathroom technique: (A) The parent puts the child into the bathroom to calm down. (B) The parent retires to the bathroom to escape from the stress and demands placed upon him by the child. (C) The parent retires to the bathroom to punish the child. (D) The parent retires to the bathroom as a way to give in to the child.

11. Who maintains control when the parent uses the bathroom technique? (A) The parent. (B) The child. (C) Neither. (D) Both parent and child.

12. What can a parent do to make the bathroom technique easier to follow through on? (A) Remove any objects that can be easily damaged by the child. (B) Remove any objects that are potentially dangerous to the child. (C) Keep in mind that if anything is broken, a consequence can be figured out later on. (D) All of the above.

13. Parents' reactions to their child's misbehavior often reinforce the behavior because: (A) They take the time to understand the reason behind the child's misbehavior. (B) It is impossible for the parents to identify their child's mistaken goal. (C) Their reaction is fulfilling the child's mistaken goal. (D) Their reaction is not fulfilling the child's mistaken goal.

14. Parents can communicate anger and irritation through: (A) Tone of voice. (B) Facial expression. (C) Eye contact. (D) All of the above.

15. Since ignoring will often decrease a child's negative behavior, what can a parent do when the child's physical well-being is involved? (A) Nothing. (B) Stop ignoring. (C) Set up a necessary precaution. (D) Allow the natural consequence to take place.

CHILD'S MISTAKEN GOALS

Consistent Misbehavior	Emotional Reaction (of parent)	Mistaken Goal	Some Corrective Measures
The showoff	Annoyed	Attention	Ignore
Walking question mark	Frustrated		Do the unexpected
Makes minor mischief	Wants to remind		Give attention at pleasant times
Bashfulness	Coaxing		Logical consequences
Instability	Delighted with "good child"		Encouragement
Fearfulness			
Anxiety			
Untidiness			
A "rebel"	Mad	Power	Remove self
Temper tantrums	Upset		Act, don't talk
Dawdling	Provoked		Be friendly
Laziness	Generally wants power		"We're all in the same boat"
Stubbornness	Challenged—"I'll *make* him do it."		Natural consequences
Disobedience	"You can't get away with it."		Encouragement
Bad habits			
Untruthfulness			
Stealing	Hurt	Revenge	Remove self
Bed wetting	"How could she do this to me?"		Win cooperation
Violent and brutal			Maintain order with minimum restraint
Sullen and defiant			Avoid retaliations
"Vicious"			Take time and effort to help child
"Violent passivity"			Encouragement
"Hopeless"	Despair—hopeless "I give up."	Inadequacy	Encouragement (may take a long time) Faith in child's ability

Part 2

Your learning activity is to complete the Parent Encouragement Chart #1.

Explanation of Chart #1

Chart #1 is designed to help parents begin encouraging themselves for not reinforcing children's misbehaviors.

It has been shown previously that a parent's reaction often encourages the child's unwanted misbehavior. Thus, the child attempts to get the parent to pay attention by whatever means works. This chart is intended to help parents monitor the number of times they are able to control their behavior and thus not feed into the child's misbehavior. For example, when a child cries to get mom to come into the bedroom, and mom stops herself from reacting, it is at that point that she should mark on her chart that she was able to do something constructive rather than feed into the child's useless need for attention.

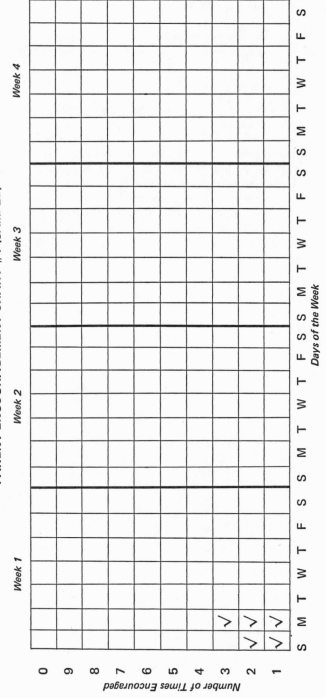

PARENT ENCOURAGEMENT CHART #1 (SAMPLE)

Number of Times Encouraged (y-axis): 0, 9, 8, 7, 6, 5, 4, 3, 2, 1

Days of the Week (x-axis): Week 1, Week 2, Week 3, Week 4

Day 1—√1. Mother refrained in the night from telling her child to stop crying and get to sleep.

√2. Mother removed herself to the bathroom during child's temper tantrum.

Day 2—√1. Mother found that she withdrew verbally/physically 3 times during child's misbehavior.

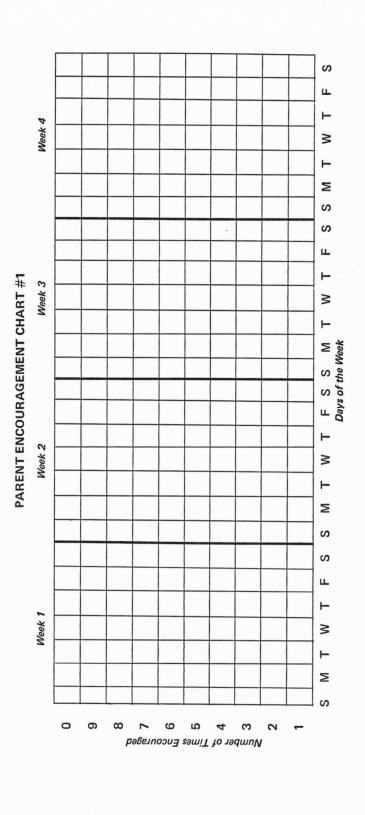

SESSION 6—POSITIVE PARENTAL ATTITUDES

Part 1

1. Readings:

    Chapter 17. Good Parents Are Allowed to Say No

            18. Children's Greatest Handicap—Overprotection

            19. Encourage Independence

            20. How to Communicate with Your Children

2. Evaluate your learning by doing the self-examination included.

Self-Examination

After you have completed your readings, try this self-examination. This will help to highlight key principles and bring into focus new ideas.

CIRCLE CORRECT ANSWER

1. The authors define good parents as those who attempt to: (A) Teach their children constructive ways of finding their place and say no only when absolutely necessary. (B) Teach their children constructive ways of finding their place along with constructive ways of dealing with life's frustrations. (C) Say no to their children whenever the parents feel like it. (D) Say no only when giving in to the children doesn't work.

2. Parents' ability to say no can teach a child to be: (A) Irresponsible. (B) Self-centered. (C) Uncooperative. (D) Cooperative.

3. In order for parents to be effective when they say no they must: (A) Be strict. (B) Be willing to back up their words with action. (C) Be apologetic when saying no. (D) Only say it when they know it won't frustrate the child.

4. The feeling that parents of exceptional children are responsible for their child being totally free of all stress and frustration is called: (A) The good parent syndrome. (B) The ideal parent. (C) The model parent. (D) The bad parent syndrome.

5. A main reason parents may overprotect a child with a physiologically handicapping condition is: (A) The child can't be taught to do anything for herself. (B) The child can't be taught her own limits of activity. (C) The parents overcompensate for their feelings of guilt. (D) The parents always know what is best for the child.

6. When parents overprotect their child, they are: (A) Showing respect for the child. (B) Placing themselves in a superior position. (C) Placing themselves in an inferior position. (D) Teaching the child a sense of independence.

7. An overprotected child commonly feels (A) Angry and resentful. (B) Appreciative and thankful. (C) Independent and self-reliant. (D) Grateful and loved.

8. Parents of exceptional children may not be encouraging independence in their child because: (A) Exceptional children usually can't learn to do things for themselves. (B) They empathize with the difficulties the child has to struggle with. (C) They pity the child for the difficulties he has to struggle with. (D) It is best to encourage dependence.

9. The difference between empathy and pity is that empathy: (A) Separates the circumstance from the person. (B) Does not separate the circumstances from the child. (C) Tends to be used when a person feels sorry for the child. (D) Usually puts the child down.

10. Which of the following is an outcome of encouraging independence in children? (A) Lack of courage. (B) Puts others in their service. (C) The development of a healthy relationship. (D) Doesn't feel OK.

11. The main responsibility given to all parents is: (A) Give their children everything they can. (B) Do everything for them. (C) Provide food and shelter. (D) Promote independence in their offspring.

12. Often parents have difficulty disciplining and communicating with their children because: (A) They put themselves in an inferior position and the child in a superior one. (B) They put themselves and the child in a superior position. (C) They put themselves in a superior position and the child in an inferior position. (D) They put themselves and the child in an inferior position.

13. Parents can communicate most effectively through the use of: (A) "I" statements. (B) "You" statements. (C) Discouraging statements. (D) "They" statements.

14. Because of the possible effects their limitations have upon communicating with others, exceptional children may rely more heavily on: (A) Verbal behavior. (B) Nonverbal behavior. (C) Talking. (D) All of the above.

15. When we verbally communicate a message to our children, our nonverbal message should: (A) Totally negate our verbal message. (B) Be totally different. (C) Totally support what was verbally said. (D) Sternly communicate that we mean business.

Communication Diagram: Mistaken Goal I—Undue Attention

Child's Misbehavior

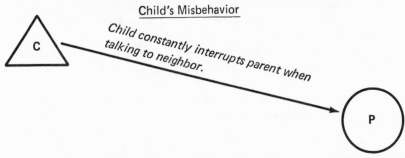

Child's message to parent is: "I need undue attention in order to feel worthwhile."

Parental Response That Reinforces Misbehavior

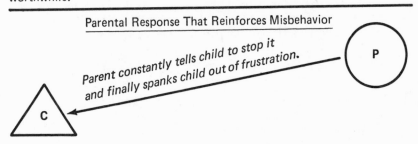

Parent's message to child is: "The more you are able to irritate and frustrate me, the more you will get my attention." (Parental response feeds into child's mistaken goal.)

Corrective Parental Response (Verbal/Nonverbal) That Diminishes Misbehavior

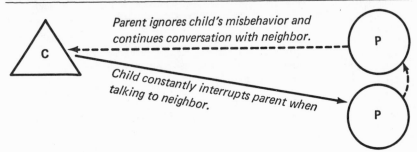

Parent's message to child is: "I will not give you my attention when you misbehave." (Parental response does not feed into child's mistaken goal.)

Part 2

Your learning activity for this phase is to complete a Communication Diagram, as shown opposite.

The following space is provided for you to graphically illustrate a Communication Diagram as shown. Refer to pp. 125, 126, 127, and 128 in chapter 20 for further illustrations of the four mistaken goals. The direction and angle of the communication will vary according to the mistaken goal. Therefore, you must draw the diagram in conjunction with the type of misbehavior exhibited by your child.

COMMUNICATION DIAGRAM #1
Mistaken Goal—

Child's Misbehavior

Child's message to parent is:

Parental Response That Reinforces Misbehavior

Parent's message to child is:

Corrective Parental Response (Verbal/Nonverbal)
That Diminishes Misbehavior

Parent's message to child is:

SESSION 7—FAMILY ATMOSPHERE

Part 1

1. Readings:
   Chapter 21. Include the Other Children
           22. Have Fun As a Family
           23. The Weekly Family Council Meeting
           24. Enjoy Your Children
2. Evaluate your learning by doing the self-examination included.

Self-Examination

After you have completed your readings, try this self-examination. This will help to highlight key principles and bring into focus new ideas.

CIRCLE CORRECT ANSWER

1. If parents of exceptional children want to create a sense of family unity and build equality among family members, they can best do this by treating: (A) The exceptional child differently. (B) The other siblings differently. (C) All the children equally. (D) All the children unequally.

2. If parents make special exceptions and overprotect their exceptional child, what often happens is: (A) The child feels superior. (B) The child may feel inferior. (C) The child feels encouraged. (D) It builds up family unity.

3. When parents take group action with their children, what often happens is it: (A) Diminishes competition between the children. (B) Breaks down family unity. (C) Increases competition between the children. (D) Makes the children feel inferior.

4. What is achieved when rules and principles are applied equally to *all* the children in the family? (A) Equality and team effort among the children. (B) An increase in competition. (C) A decrease in motivation. (D) An increase in negative attention-getting behavior.

5. The most important function of family fun time is to encourage: (A) The family to become a more cohesive group. (B) An increase in laughter in the family. (C) People not to think about their problems. (D) Competitiveness among individual members of the family to win.

6. In order for the exceptional child to participate fully in family fun time we should: (A) Let her do anything she wants. (B) Play only games

she likes. (C) Coordinate her limitations with the activity. (D) All of the above.

7. Excluding the exceptional child from family fun activities promotes: (A) More family unity. (B) The exceptional child's belief of being different. (C) A sense of equality. (D) Doesn't make any difference.

8. In the family council, the democratic problem-solving process used to make decisions is: (A) Consensus. (B) Parental authority. (C) Authority of chairperson. (D) Majority rule.

9. The use of consensus in the family council helps the exceptional child feel: (A) Inferior. (B) In control. (C) Special. (D) Equal.

10. When should family council meetings be held? (A) Whenever possible. (B) On a weekly basis. (C) When problems arise. (D) Once a month.

11. The one major advantage of the use of the family council for the other children is: (A) Parents don't have to do anything. (B) Children suffer the consequences of their actions. (C) Children have a sense of belonging by sharing their ideas. (D) A forum is provided for criticizing the exceptional child.

12. Decisions made at the family council are: (A) Established permanently. (B) Good only if all members are present. (C) Are subject to parental approval. (D) In effect until the next council meeting.

13. Parental perfection is: (A) A must for good parenting. (B) An impossible task. (C) Only natural. (D) Necessary in dealing with exceptional children.

14. Parents who put off acknowledging their own personal needs: (A) Diminish their effectiveness as parents. (B) Exhibit a necessary characteristic of a responsible parent. (C) Are effective parents. (D) Create a positive relationship between themselves and their children.

15. When parents are able to relax around their children, they: (A) Enhance independence and responsibility in their children. (B) Enjoy their children more. (C) Allow their children to enjoy life more. (D) All of the above.

Part 2

Keep up the good work. For your learning activity this session we would like you to continue to encourage your children.

We have included an additional encouragement chart to record your encouragement toward your children. (Chart #1 is the same as in chart #3, session 3.)

We would also like you to initiate your first family council meeting, utilizing chart #2.

Review before and evaluate immediately after first family council.

ENCOURAGEMENT CHART #1

Child's Name:

Child's Name:

Child's Name:

Child's Name:

Number of Times Encouraged

0
9
8
7
6
5
4
3
2
1

S M T W T F S S M T W T F S S M T W T F S S M T W T F S

Days of the Week

CHART #2
Family Council Checklist

Answer the following questions.	√ Yes	√ No
1. Was there consensus of agreement?		
2. Was consistent time and day mutually agreed upon?		
3. Was one meeting kept reasonably short in time and positive in nature?		
4. Was attendance of all family members encouraged?		
5. Was the purpose and general rules discussed at meeting?		
6. Was family fun time activity planned at initial meeting?		
7. Were the issues discussed of a common family concern?		
8. Was it a positive problem-solving discussion?		
9. Were appropriate procedures taken to include exceptional child?		
10. Did parents allow their children equal participation?		

SESSION 8—REEXAMINING YOUR GOALS

Part 1

This session was set up for you to reexamine the family and child goals you established in session 1. Reexamine the goals in terms of progress made and further areas you wish to work on. Use chart #1 to record your progress and further areas for remedial action.

Part 2

Your active participation in creating a pleasant home life and in guiding your children toward useful and constructive behavior has just begun. It may be easy for you to slip back into your old ways, so you must constantly check yourself from time to time. Remain consistent in your child-rearing practices and continually use encouragement.

The knowledge and experience you have gained in the past weeks are tools of *prevention.* Children will always misbehave, but now you have what it takes to "nip it in the bud." Your children will greatly appreciate all the time you have dedicated to helping make your family a better place to live.

CHART #1
Reexamining Your Goals

Briefly list your original goals.	What progress has been made?
1.	1.
2.	2.
3.	3.
4.	4.
What areas need further work?	*How will you work on these?*
1.	1.
2.	2.
3.	3.
4.	4.
5.	5.

SELF-EXAMINATION QUIZ ANSWERS
(WITH PAGE REFERENCES)

Session 2	Session 3
1. D, page 6	1. B, page 42
2. A, page 3	2. C, page 42
3. A, page 6	3. D, page 45
4. B, page 8	4. A, page 49
5. D, page 8	5. A, page 40
6. D, page 10	6. C, page 49
7. B, page 17	7. C, page 49
8. B, page 15	8. D, page 50
9. A, page 12	9. B, page 56
10. A, page 16	10. A, page 54
11. C, page 16	11. D, page 62
12. D, page 23	12. B, page 65
13. C, page 22, 24	13. C, page 67
14. D, pages 30, 31, 32, 33	14. A, page 67
15. C, page 34	15. C, page 69

Session 5	Session 6	Session 7
1. D, page 73	1. B, page 102	1. C, page 134
2. D, page 73	2. D, page 102	2. B, page 134
3. B, page 77	3. B, page 105	3. A, page 135
4. B, page 79	4. A, page 102	4. A, page 135
5. C, pages 78, 79	5. C, page 107	5. A, page 137
6. B, page 85	6. B, page 107	6. C, page 138
7. B, page 81	7. A, page 108	7. B, page 137, 138
8. C, page 85	8. C, page 111	8. A, page 142
9. D, page 84	9. A, page 112	9. D, page 142
10. B, page 89	10. C, page 112	10. B, page 142
11. A, page 90	11. D, page 110	11. C, page 144
12. D, page 91	12. C, page 117, 118	12. D, page 145
13. C, page 92	13. A, page 118	13. B, page 147
14. D, page 95	14. B, page 123	14. A, page 148
15. C, page 96	15. C, page 120	15. D, page 148

APPENDIX 2

A PARENT STUDY GROUP USING
RAISING THE EXCEPTIONAL CHILD

The idea of parent study groups was originally developed for use with the book *Children: The Challenge* by Vicki Soltz in her *Study Group Leader's Manual* (Chicago: Alfred Adler Institute, 1967). Since then, parent study groups have grown in popularity, and *A Parents' Guide to Children: The Challenge* (New York: Hawthorn, 1978) was written to provide parents and study group leaders with a systematic nine-week course of study using *Children: The Challenge*.

Now, with the writing of this book, *Raising the Exceptional Child*, parent study groups can be specifically geared to the needs of parents of exceptional children. Parents and study group leaders can use the following material to help you in the orientation of your parent study group. During the very first meeting of your group you should review the introductory guidelines and comments. Then move on to appendix 1 and review the material presented for session 1 during the first meeting. From then on, follow the order of sessions and material presented: session 2 to be covered in the second meeting, session 3 in the third, and so on.

At the end of this appendix is an evaluation form, which you can fill out at the end of your parent study group course to weigh the benefits you have experienced from the group.

The material presented in this appendix has been adapted from *A Parents' Guide to Children: The Challenge* (New York: Hawthorn Books, 1978).

188

INTRODUCTION TO YOUR PARENT STUDY GROUP

The first meeting is intended for you to become acquainted with one another and your group's purpose. To initiate discussion, take some time to read the articles that follow:

1. The philosophy of parent study groups
2. How your parent study group will run
3. The ground rules of your parent study group

Remember—assignments 1 through 3 are for your discussion. It is your responsibility to contribute by asking questions and by making suggestions if you feel that they are appropriate.

THE PHILOSOPHY OF PARENT STUDY GROUPS

We are living in a constantly changing society that no longer has a tradition of child rearing. All parents are faced with the task of rearing their children to become the most independent and self-sufficient individuals possible. However, the task of parenting has increased in difficulty due to societal changes and the lack of traditions. Your parent study group (PSG) will aid you in achieving these goals by educating you in democratic principles of family living, which are congruent with society's movement toward equality.

You will join together with other parents of exceptional children to share ideas and discover with each other that your situations are experienced by many families. You may also be fortunate enough to learn that it is not necessary to live with the many misbehaviors considered only natural for exceptional children. This can become a reality when you learn the *purpose* of children's misbehavior and effective ways of encouraging *positive* behavior. Emphasis is also placed upon understanding how your child's handicap does or does not affect misbehavior and how to develop an atmosphere of mutual respect in your home.

Building cooperation, mutual respect, and skill in diminishing misbehavior—along with skill to increase proper behavior—in children is not easily accomplished. However, receiving support and encouragement from other parents can ease the task and increase your positive experiences. Your PSG follows a clear and simple approach, which will allow you to gain an understanding of children and the knowledge to guide children away from useless behavior and toward useful behavior.

Dealing with present difficulties common in most families with exceptional children (e.g., fighting between children, bickering at mealtime, temper tantrums) is only one aspect of your PSG. The knowledge that you as a parent can gain is a tool of prevention. Only when you, the parent, truly understand your child's motivation can you then lend constructive guidance, which will move you beyond dealing with present difficulties toward anticipating and forestalling future problems.

HOW YOUR PSG WILL RUN

1. Your PSG will run for eight weeks, meeting once a week for an hour and a half.

2. The principles that will be discussed follow the Adlerian philosophy of family living, as presented in this book.

3. At each weekly meeting, you will discuss the homework, along with the principles and issues brought out in the assigned chapters for that particular week. Don't get nervous, the readings are short and they make sense.

4. Your PSG leader is there to initiate discussion, *not to lecture,* therefore your *verbal* participation is crucial. The more you ask questions and discuss the readings, the more you and your group will learn.

5. There will be times when you wish to discuss a situation occurring in your family. Knowing how to present your situation to your group is important. They need to know

   A. What happened? State briefly.

   B. Names and ages of children involved.

   C. What did you do?

   D. How did you feel?

   E. Child's disability.

Gaining an understanding of your situation and how to improve it is as simple as A, B, C, D, E.

6. Finally, do you have any questions? Don't be afraid to ask a question. You may be helping another parent in your group who has the same question.

GROUND RULES

1. I realize that this is *my* parent study group. What I get out of my group depends upon the amount of time and energy I put in.

2. I realize that there may be ideas presented in my group that I won't agree with. That's OK. What I wish to use and take from the group is up to me. If there is something I don't understand or agree with, I will bring it up at our next meeting. However, it is up to me not to get into a power struggle with the leader or other group members. I am interested in learning new ideas, not in disputing.

3. I realize that all reading and homework assignments must be done for each week. This helps assure me of getting the most out of my group. It would be unfair of me to depend solely upon other members to have done the assignment so I can learn from them. We all must share in the responsibility for learning.

4. I realize that the group leader will be a guide for discussion but that I, too, have equal responsibility to participate in the discussion. I am aware that other parents can learn from me, as I can learn from them.

5. Punctuality and regular attendance are very important to the operation of my group. Indifference to these is disrespectful to group members, and I would like to expect equal consideration from them. I also realize that by being late and missing meetings, I will lose out on valuable learning, which will hinder my success.

6. Confidentiality is extremely important. Parents often share situations that are going on in their own families that are personal in nature. I agree not to discuss with anyone outside of the group personal situations that a member has brought up.

7. To expect miracles or instant behavior changes from my children is unrealistic. When I learn a new method, I will not try it *until I am sure I understand it*. I want to use these methods to build harmonious relationships with my children—not to manipulate or dominate them. I will not tell other parents how they should raise their children. If my spouse does not agree with the new methods I'm learning, I will not try to win him or her over by arguing. Successful demonstration works better than words.

EVALUATION OF YOUR PSG AND GROUP LEADER

1. Did you accomplish your goal? Yes _____ No _____

2. Did you accomplish more _____ or less _____ than you expected?

Explain: _____

_____

3. What did you find to be the most helpful? _____

    Explain: _____ _____

_____

4. What was the least helpful? _____

_____

5. Do you feel the group leader helped to stimulate group discussion?
    Yes _____ No _____

6. Do you have any ideas to improve the course? Explain: _____

_____

APPENDIX 3

LIST OF NATIONAL ORGANIZATIONS

Academy of Dentistry for
  Handicapped
Division of Pedodontics
School of Dentistry
University of California
San Francisco, Calif. 94143

Alexander Graham Bell
  Association for the Deaf
1537 35th St., N.W.
Washington, D.C. 20007

Allergy Foundation of America
801 Second Ave.
New York, N.Y. 10017

American Academy for Cerebral
  Palsy
1255 New Hampshire Ave., N.W.
Washington, D.C. 20036

American Academy of Pediatrics
1801 Hinman Ave.
Evanston, Ill. 60204

American Allergy Academy
611 E. Wells St.
Milwaukee, Wisc. 53202

American Alliance for Health,
  Physical Education and Recreation
1201 16th St., N.W.
Washington, D.C. 20036

American Association of Workers
  for the Blind
1511 K St., Rm. 637
Washington, D.C. 20005

American Association on Mental
  Deficiency
5201 Connecticut Ave., N.W.
Washington, D.C. 20015

American Athletic Association of the
  Deaf, Inc.
2851 West St. Tropaz Ave.
Tucson, Ariz. 85713

American Cancer Society, Inc.
219 E. 42nd St.
New York, N.Y. 10017

American Coalition of Citizens with
  Disabilities
1346 Connecticut Ave., N.W.,
  Suite 817
Washington, D.C. 20036

American Council of the Blind
1211 Connecticut Ave., N.W.,
  Suite 506
Washington, D.C. 20036

American Diabetes Association, Inc.
600 Fifth Ave.
New York, N.Y. 10020

American Foundation for Autistic
  Children
4510 Cumberland Ave.
Chevy Chase, Md. 20015

American Foundation for the Blind
15 W. 16th St.
New York, N.Y. 10011

American Heart Association
7320 Greenville Ave.
Dallas, Texas 75231

American Lung Association
1740 Broadway
New York, N.Y. 10019

American Medical Association
535 N. Dearborn St.
Chicago, Ill. 60610

The American Occupational
  Therapy Association, Inc.
6000 Executive Blvd., Suite 200
Rockville, Md. 20852

American Orthotic and Prosthetic
  Association
1444 N St., N.W.
Washington, D.C. 20005

American Physical Therapy
  Association
1156 15th St., N.W., Suite 500
Washington, D.C. 20005

American Podiatry Association
20 Chevy Chase Circle, N.W.
Washington, D.C. 20015

American Printing House for the
  Blind, Inc.
1839 Frankfort Ave.
Louisville, Ky. 40206

The American Psychiatric
  Association
Office of Government Relations
1700 18th St., N.W.
Washington, D.C. 20009

American Psychological Association
1200 17th St., N.W.
Washington, D.C. 20036

American Schizophrenia Association
1114 First Ave.
New York, N.Y. 10021

American Speech and
  Hearing Association
9030 Old Georgetown Rd.
Washington, D.C. 20014

The Arthritis Foundation
475 Riverside Dr., Room 240
New York, N.Y. 10027

Association for Children with
Learning Disabilities
5225 Grace St.
Pittsburgh, Pa. 15236

Association for the Education of the
Visually Handicapped
919 Walnut St.
Philadelphia, Pa. 19107

Association of University
Affiliated Facilities
1100 17th St., N.W., Suite 908
Washington, D.C. 20036

Brain Research Foundation
University of Chicago
343 S. Dearborn St.
Chicago, Ill. 60604

Child Welfare League of America
1346 Connecticut Ave., N.W.,
Rm. 310
Washington, D.C. 20036

Council for Children with
Behavioral Disorders
University of Minnesota
150 Pillsbury Dr., Rm. 103
Minneapolis, Minn. 55455

The Council for Exceptional
Children
1920 Association Dr.
Reston, Va. 22091

Council of Spanish-Speaking
Mental Health Organizations
1725 K St., N.W., Suite 1201
Washington, D.C. 20036

Cystic Fibrosis Foundation
3379 Peachtree Rd., N.E.
Atlanta, Georgia 30326

Deafness Research Foundation
366 Madison Ave.
New York, N.Y. 10017

Developmental Disabilities Law
Project
University of Maryland Law School
500 W. Baltimore St.
Baltimore, Md. 21201

Disability Law Rights Center
1446 Connecticut Ave., N.W.
Washington, D.C. 20036

Disability Rights Center
1346 Connecticut Ave., N.W.,
Suite 1124
Washington, D.C. 20036

Downs Syndrome Congress
8509 Wagon Wheel Rd.
Alexandria, Va. 22309

Epilepsy Foundation of America
1828 L St., N.W.
Washington, D.C. 20036

Federation of the Handicapped, Inc.
211 W. 14th St.
New York, N.Y. 10011

52 Association
147 E. 50th St.
New York, N.Y. 10022

Goodwill Industries of America
9200 Wisconsin Ave.
Washington, D.C. 20014

International Association of Parents
for the Deaf
814 Thayer Ave.
Silver Spring, Md. 20910

International Association of
Rehabilitation, Inc.
5530 Wisconsin Ave., N.W.,
Suite 955
Washington, D.C. 20015

International Handicapped Net
P.O. Box B
San Gabriel, Calif. 91778

Leukemia Society of America, Inc.
211 E. 43rd St.
New York, N.Y. 10017

Library of Congress Division for
the Blind and Physically
Handicapped
1291 Taylor St., N.W.
Washington, D.C. 20542

The Menninger Foundation
Box 829
Topeka, Kans. 66601

Mental Disability Law Reporter
1800 M St., N.W.
Washington, D.C. 20036

Muscular Dystrophy Association of
America
810 Seventh Ave.
New York, N.Y. 10019

Myasthemia Gravis Foundation, Inc.
230 Park Ave.
New York, N.Y. 10017

National Accreditation Council for
Agencies Serving the Blind and
Visually Handicapped
79 Madison Ave., Rm. 1406
New York, N.Y. 10016

National Amputation Foundation
12–45 150th St.
Whitestone, N.Y. 11357

National Apostolate for the
Mentally Retarded
P.O. Box 4588
Trinity College
Washington, D.C. 20017

National Association for Down's
Syndrome
P.O. Box 63
Oak Park, Ill. 60303

National Association for Mental
Health
1800 N. Kent St.
Arlington, Va. 22209

National Association for
Retarded Citizens
2709 Ave. E, E.
P.O. Box 6109
Arlington, Texas 76011

National Association for Visually
Handicapped
305 E. 24th St.
New York, N.Y. 10010

National Association of Coordinators
of State Programs for the
Mentally Retarded
2001 Jefferson Davis Hgwy.,
Suite 1010
Arlington, Va. 22202

National Association of the Deaf
814 Thayer Ave.
Silver Spring, Md. 20910

National Association of the
Deaf and Blind
2703 Forest Oak Circle
Norman, Okla. 73071

National Association of Hearing
and Speech Action
814 Thayer Ave.
Silver Spring, Md. 20910

National Association of Parents of
the Deaf and Blind
2703 Forest Oak Circle
Norman, Okla. 73071

National Association of the
Physically Handicapped
2810 Perrace Rd., S.E., Apt. A465
Washington, D.C. 20020

National Association of Private
Psychiatric Hospitals
1701 K St., N.W., Suite 31205
Washington, D.C. 20006

National Association of Private
Residential Facilities for the
Mentally Retarded
6269 Leesburg Pike, Suite B5
Falls Church, Va. 22044

National Association of State
Directors of Special Education
1201 16th St., N.W., Suite 610E
Washington, D.C. 20036

National Association of State Mental
Health Program Directors
1001 Third St., S.W.
Washington, D.C. 20034

National Center for a Barrier Free
Environment
8401 Connecticut Ave., Suite 402
Chevy Chase, Md. 20015

National Center for Law and
the Deaf
Seventh and Florida Avenues, N.E.
Washington, D.C. 20002

National Center for Law and the
Handicapped
1235 N. Eddy St.
South Bend, Ind. 46617

National Council of Organizations
for Children and Youth
1910 K St., N.W.
Washington, D.C. 20006

National Easter Seal Society for
Crippled Children and Adults
2023 W. Ogden Ave.
Chicago, Ill. 60612

National Epilepsy League
6 N. Michigan Ave.
Chicago, Ill. 60602

National Federation of the
Blind, Inc.
1346 Connecticut Ave., N.W.,
Suite 212
Washington, D.C. 20036

National Federation of Business and
Professional Women's Clubs
2012 Massachusetts Ave., N.W.
Washington, D.C. 20032

National Foundation of Dentistry for
the Handicapped
1121 Broadway, Suite 5
Boulder, Colo. 80302

National Foundation/March of
Dimes
1275 Mamaroneck Ave.
White Plains, N.Y. 10605

National Foundation/March of
Dimes
1707 H St., N.W.
Washington, D.C. 20006

National Fraternal Society of
Deaf
1300 W. Northwest Hgwy.
Mt. Prospect, Ill. 60056

National Genetics Foundation
9 W. 57th St.
New York, N.Y. 10019

The National Hemophilia Foundation
25 W. 39th St.
New York, N.Y. 10018

National Industries for the Blind
2020 Jericho Turnpike
New Hyde Park, N.Y. 11040

National Industries for the
Severely Handicapped
4350 East-West Hgwy., Suite 1120
Washington, D.C. 20014

National Kidney Foundation
116 E. 27th St., 5th Fl.
New York, N.Y. 10016

National Multiple Sclerosis
Society
205 E. 42nd St.
New York, N.Y. 10017

National Paraplegia Foundation
333 N. Michigan Ave.
Chicago, Ill. 60601

National Rehabilitation Association
1522 K St., N.W.
Washington, D.C. 20005

National Retinitis Pigmentosa
Foundation, Inc.
8331 Mindale Circle
Baltimore, Md. 21207

National Self Help Clearing House
Health Complex
Pomona, N.Y. 10470

National Society for Autistic
Children, Inc.
169 Tampa Ave.
Albany, N.Y. 12208

National Society for the
Prevention of Blindness, Inc.
79 Madison Ave.
New York, N.Y. 10016

National Technical Institute for
the Deaf
One Lomb Memorial Dr.
Rochester, N.Y. 14623

National Therapeutic Recreation
Society (NRPA)
1601 N. Kent Street
Arlington, Va. 22209

North American Riding for the
Handicapped Association, Inc.
R.R. 1, Box 171
Augusta, Mich. 49012

Parkinson's Disease Foundation
640 W. 168th St.
New York, N.Y. 10032

Professional Rehabilitation Workers
with Adult Deaf, Inc.
814 Thayer Ave.
Silver Spring, Md. 20910

Rehabilitation International USA
20 W. 40th St.
New York, N.Y. 10018

Registry of Interpreters for
the Deaf
P.O. Box 1339
Washington, D.C. 20013

Damon Runyon Memorial Fund for
Cancer Research
33 West 56th Street
New York, N.Y. 10019

Sertoma Foundation
750 Montclair Rd.
Birmingham, Ala. 35213

Society for the Rehabilitation of
the Facially Disfigured, Inc.
550 First Ave.
New York, N.Y. 10016

Special Olympics, Inc.
1701 K St., N.W., Suite 202
Washington, D.C. 20006

United Cerebral Palsy Association
66 E. 34th St.
New York, N.Y. 10016

United Ostomy Association, Inc.
111 Wilshire Blvd.
Los Angeles, Calif. 90017

Western Law Center for the
Handicapped
849 S. Broadway
Los Angeles, Calif. 90014

APPENDIX 4

SUGGESTED READINGS

The Special Child Handbook, Joan McNamara and Bernard McNamara (New York: Hawthorn Books, 1977). Factual and supportive information to parents of exceptional children to maximize the resources known to the parents.

Logical Consequences: A New Approach to Discipline, Rudolf Dreikurs and Loren Grey (New York: Hawthorn Books, 1968). Entire book is devoted to the use of logical consequences as an alternative corrective measure for children's misbehavior.

Children: The Challenge, Rudolf Dreikurs and Vicki Soltz (New York: Hawthorn Books, 1964). One of the most widely recognized child-rearing texts, which fully describes democratic child-rearing practices.

A Parents' Guide to Children: The Challenge, Lawrence Zuckerman, Valerie Zuckerman, Rebecca Costa, and Michael T. Yura (New York: Hawthorn Books, 1978). Helps structure the information given in Children: The Challenge to increase the effectiveness of the techniques presented.

How to Stop Fighting with Your Kids, Rudolf Dreikurs, Shirley Gould, and Raymond Corsini (New York: Ace Books, 1974). Heavy emphasis upon the implementation of the family council and provides many illustrations.

INDEX

Accidents (of child), 39, 51
Actions vs. words, 56, 78, 83–87
  "parent deaf" children, 41–42,
    87
  saying no and acting on it, 59,
    84, 105
Anger (of child)
  and communication, 117–120
  and overprotection, 108, 109,
    112
Anger (of parents)
  and communication, 122
  and mistaken goals of child, 93,
    124, 129
  and overprotection, 28
  as problem when implementing
    logical consequences, 56, 57,
    60, 62, 63
  in power struggle, 41, 42, 63,
    161, 175
Anxiety (attention getting), 161,
    175
Asking questions (attention get-
    ting), 161, 175
Attention getting (by child), 12–13,
    18, 38–39
  behavior pattern, 79, 161, 175

Attention getting (by child), (*cont.*)
  and communication, 128, 180
  corrective measures, 42, 90, 175
  parents' reaction, 38–39, 44, 161
    See also Goals (of child),
    mistaken
Attention getting (by siblings),
    30–31
  imitation, 33–34
  overcompensation, 33

Bashfulness (attention getting),
    161, 175
Bathroom technique (parental
    withdrawal), 88–91, 95
Bed wetting (revenge), 161, 175
Behavior/misbehavior
  behavior patterns, 8–16, 21–25
    See also Individual patterns
  characteristics of specific handi-
    caps, 15, 17–20, 38
  consistency a factor in change,
    76–80, 84
  cooperation fostered by child's
    independence, 112
  correction should start early, 81–
    82